100 PLANTS

for

EASY TO MAINTAIN
Gardens

100 PLANTS

for

EASY TO MAINTAIN

Gardens

General Editor: Mary Moody

CRESCENT BOOKS

NEW YORK • AVENEL

Contributing writers: Mary Moody, Stephanie Watson

Published by Lansdowne Publishing Pty Ltd
Level 5, 70 George Street, Sydney NSW 2000, Australia

This 1995 edition published by Crescent Books,
distributed by Random House Value Publishing, Inc.,
40 Engelhard Avenue, Avenel, New Jersey 07001

Random House
New York • Toronto • London • Sydney • Auckland

First published 1994

Managing Director: Jane Curry
Publishing Manager: Deborah Nixon
Production Manager: Sally Stokes
Project Coordinators/Editors: Kate Oliver and Bronwyn Hilton
Copy Editor: Glenda Downing
Horticultural Advisor: Liz Ball
Design Concept: Catherine Martin
Typesetter: Veronica Hilton
Formatted in Galliard on Quark Xpress
Printed in Singapore by Kyodo Printing Co (S'pore) Pte Ltd

ISBN 0-517-12127-1

A CIP catalog record for this book is available from the Library of Congress.

KEY TO SYMBOLS

○	prefers full sun
◑	prefers partial shade
●	prefers shade
p$\overset{\vee}{\text{H}}$	acid soil
$\overset{\wedge}{\text{p}}$H	alkaline soil
❖	half-hardy – temperatures down to 0°C
❖❖	hardy – temperatures down to -5°C
❖❖❖	fully hardy – temperatures down to -15°C

Contents

Introduction

✿ **THE EASE OF MAINTENANCE DREAM** In theory, our gardens should be a haven; a place to escape from all the daily hassles of life, to sit and enjoy the pleasures of nature. It seems logical, therefore, that we should endeavour to create a garden that will not require many hours of painstaking toil bogged down with routine tasks such as weeding, mowing, edge-trimming, and watering.

Many gardens become a source of frustration for their owners, especially when the plants they select fail to thrive, or pests and disease infestations become a major problem. However, by selecting the right plants and taking time initially to design the garden layout carefully, a low-maintenance garden can be easily attained. For many people, the term 'low-maintenance' is indicative of gardens that are simply trees and shrubs surrounded by lawns. Yet this style of garden can still take hours of work each week, especially during spring and summer when lawns grow so rapidly. Keeping grass well groomed and free from weeds can be troublesome, and perhaps lawn should be avoided altogether in a truly maintenance-free garden. Instead, consider well-mulched beds of trees, shrubs, perennials, and bulbs, with ground covers that will eventually fill the gaps between larger species and reduce ground work altogether. Creating a garden of this type may involve rethinking your notions about how a garden should look. Abandon the idea of neat flower borders and well-tended vegetable plots. Instead, think of a more casual approach, with less eye for detail. For example, cottage and woodland gardens usually achieve a deliberately 'unplanned' appearance, but this can take quite a deal of design and planning to create. Once established, however, these gardens tend to take care of themselves, as annuals self-seed each season and perennials and bulbs emerge from beneath the soil surface to surprise and delight.

✿ **THE SECRET OF MULCHING** The routine task of weeding is a tremendous time-waster in the garden. It is possible to avoid the task of battling weed infestations that threaten to overwhelm young plants, by simply mulching thickly between them before weeds have an opportunity to take root. What is mulch? In nature, plants grow together in harmony, helping each other to survive (or competing and wiping each other out completely!) In natural environments, leaves and bark from overhead trees and large shrubs fall to the ground and create a thick layer of organic matter that is very beneficial to the lower-growing species. This layer of organic matter is called a mulch, and we should make use of it in the garden to re-create the balance found in more natural environments. Indeed, mulching has a great many benefits and is the essential secret of a successful low-maintenance garden. A well-mulched garden requires less watering in summer, and the soil temperature is more evenly maintained. If organic mulches are used then plants will be supplied with a steady quantity of nutrients, reducing the necessity for regular feeding. The best mulches are well-rotted manures and homemade compost, although straw, grass clippings, and leaf mulch can also be used. Ideally, a combination of all these mulches will give the best results, with a sprinkling of blood and bone thrown in for good measure. This helps the mulch to break down, and adds to the feeding benefits. Begin by layering manure at ground level, then top this with a mixture of straw and leaves or grass clippings and leaves. As the mulch layers break down, they can be replenished, to ensure continuous protection from weeds.

Certain plants resent being mulched around the base of their stem or trunk, so avoid piling organic matter above ground level. In the case of young seedlings, thick mulch at the base will create very humid conditions, which can cause the stems to rot. Simply leave a gap between the base of the plant and the mulch to allow free air circulation.

✿ **SELECTING THE RIGHT PLANTS** Species selected for a low-maintenance garden must be vigorous and hardy, chosen for their ability to thrive without a lot of fuss and attention. Avoid plants that require regular spraying, watering, and feeding; or those that need to be routinely pruned. Look for varieties that are growing successfully in nearby gardens, as these have a proven track record in the local soil and climate conditions. Do not attempt to grow exotic species that have different requirements to the ones that occur naturally in your garden—only adventurous gardeners with time to spend nurturing difficult plants should undertake such a task.

Trees, shrubs, and perennial plants will always require less maintenance than annual varieties, which need to be planted out, fed, and watered routinely. Plants in containers also need lots of care and attention, so avoid them unless you have time to spare.

When visiting the nursery in search of suitable species, always look for healthy specimens and transplant them into the garden immediately. Plants left too long in nursery pots will lose condition, and probably never recover after planting. Spend some time preparing the soil prior to planting, as this will also ensure long-term success and prevent later time-consuming problems. Water the ground well the day before planting, and incorporate lots of organic matter, such as homemade composts and well-rotted manures, to improve the soil fertility and texture.

The plants selected in this book have been chosen for their ease of cultivation. Once established in the right soil, in the correct situation these plants should require very little further care and attention, and will provide the gardener with many years of enjoyment. While some have quite particular requirements in terms of soil, drainage, or sunlight, if these requirements are met, they will be very easy to maintain.

❀ **GARDEN DESIGN IS ALSO IMPORTANT** When laying out the garden avoid overcrowding, although this is a common temptation when plants are small. Establish the mature height and spread of each species, then allow plenty of space for it to grow and reach its potential. While overlapping looks pretty and is acceptable, overcrowding will cause plenty of problems at a later stage, as plants invariably fail to thrive in these conditions. A lot of time is wasted cutting out plants that have become overwhelmed by others, or that have become weak and unhealthy in a crowded environment. Again, the time spent initially planning the garden will prevent ongoing maintenance problems.

If the garden has some areas of lawn, ensure that these areas have edgings or borders that do not require trimming. A simple mowing strip at ground level will mean that the lawnmower can reach right to the edge, without any further trimming requires. Spaded edges also need little ongoing attention and are therefore practical in a low-maintenance scheme. In areas where watering is essential, consider installing a simple watering system to save time and water. Although automatic watering systems are best put into place before the garden is planted out, the newer, all-plastic watering kits are quite simple to place in an established garden. Indeed, they are easy enough for the average gardener to set up without professional help, which is a great cost saving. Small sprinklers or ground-level drip systems take water to the base of the plants where it is needed, rather than spraying it into the general area, which often happens with movable sprinkler systems. In summer, an automatic timer can be attached to the tap, turning on the sprinklers in the later afternoon. Here there is a danger of overwatering, which can happen when automatic sprinklers are activated when it is raining. This not only wastes water, but leeches valuable nutrients from the soil. Simply monitor the daily watering to get the best results from the system.

❁ HOW TO USE THIS BOOK

This book has been designed as a simple guide to successfully cultivating all the plants listed. The soil pH level has been specified only when it needs to be either acid or alkaline, according to the particular requirements of the plant. All other plants can be easily grown in soil in the neutral range (that is, pH 7.0). Refer to the key to symbols on page 4.

A plant's preference for sun, partial shade or full shade, and its hardiness rating are also indicated by symbols. The hardiness symbols indicate each individual plant's ability to withstand winter temperatures and frost. No symbols have been given for annuals, which are only grown from spring to autumn in cool and cold climates, and therefore are not expected to survive winter.

The mature height of plants, indicated under 'Description', may vary from one climate to another, sometimes only reaching the maximum size in the country in which it is a native species.

Where advice has been given on pests and disease infestations, this is meant as a guide to a certain plant's susceptibility to a particular problem. Treatment of that problem will vary from one country to another.

Acer palmatum

Japanese maple ○ ◑ ❖❖❖

✿ **DESCRIPTION** Few deciduous trees can rival the unique beauty of the Japanese maple, with its spectacular autumn foliage and graceful habit. It is a popular but slow-growing tree, reaching 15 feet (4.5 m) after 20 years with a spread of 10 feet (3 m). Although a number of cultivars have been developed, the original species has bright green, palmate leaves with deeply incised margins. They offer a wealth of hues in autumn, including orange, red, and yellow. During spring, clusters of small, purplish-pink flowers adorn the tree, followed by characteristic winged seeds. ✿ **PLANTING** Japanese maples prefer an open position with protection from strong winds and the harsh afternoon sun. Taller trees will often provide the necessary protection. The soil should be rich, moist and well drained and can be supplemented with organic matter at planting time. Autumn and spring are the best seasons to plant a Japanese maple, although it is wise to make your purchase when the autumn tones can be observed. ✿ **FLOWERING** Small blooms emerge en mass in mid-spring. ✿ **CULTIVATION** Pruning is rarely necessary and should be limited to the removal of dead or damaged branches during winter. Mulch generously to retain the soil's moisture. ✿ **PROPAGATION** By stratified seed sown as soon as it is ripe.

Aesculus glabra
Ohio buckeye ○ ◐ ❖❖❖

✿ **DESCRIPTION** The Ohio buckeye is a popular specimen tree that is often featured in streetscapes, parks, and large gardens of the northern hemisphere. Prominent, orange, autumn foliage is what makes this deciduous tree so desirable, as the fruits are inedible and the timber is not utilized commercially. It prefers a cool climate and may reach a height of 20 to 30 feet (6 to 9 m) with a similar spread. During spring, boldly veined leaves appear along with panicles of green to yellow flowers. These are promptly followed by rounded and prickly seed capsules. ✿ **PLANTING** Choose a site with deep, moist soil and plenty of room for the tree to grow. Plant from autumn to spring in full sun or light shade in a location with protection from drying winds. ✿ **FLOWERING** Flower spikes appear during spring. ✿ **CULTIVATION** The Ohio buckeye is not at all tolerant of drought, so water deeply throughout summer and thickly mulch the surrounding soil. When allowed to dry out, the leaves develop unsightly brown edges and drop prematurely. Prune young trees to shape during early spring and watch for any signs of leaf spot. Established trees can, for the most part, be left to their own devices. ✿ **PROPAGATION** By seed in autumn.

Cercis siliquastrum
Judas tree ○ pH ❖❖❖

❀ **DESCRIPTION** Old legends claim that the Judas tree inherited its name when Judas hanged himself from one in shame. Despite its tainted history, this bushy, deciduous tree is still a favourite amongst gardeners worldwide, with its attractive clusters of rose-pink, pea-shaped blossoms that cover the bare branches from late spring through to late summer. (White and deep purple cultivars are also available.) Soon to follow are the bright green, heart-shaped leaves and long, reddish-brown seed pods. Judas trees are slow growing, but may eventually reach a height of 20 feet (6 m) in cultivation.
❀ **PLANTING** Select a sunny position with deep, well-drained soil that is slightly alkaline in pH. Judas trees detest any form of root disturbance, so they are best planted when small in size. Spring or autumn is the best time to do this.❀ **FLOWERING** A mass of stalkless blooms appear from late spring through to summer depending on the climate. ❀ **CULTIVATION** Young trees require protection from severe frosts. Cultivation around the root zone is best avoided. Mulch the tree well to reduce the need for weeding, and water deeply throughout summer. Pruning is not necessary except for the removal of dead wood. ❀ **PROPAGATION** By scarified seed in autumn or early spring.

Crataegus monogyna

English hawthorn ○ ◐ ❖❖❖

✿ **OTHER NAMES** May thorn, Common hawthorn

✿ **DESCRIPTION** The English hawthorn is commonly grown as a hedgerow plant throughout Europe. Its dense, twiggy branches and unforgiving thorns have been used for centuries to keep intruders out, and grazing animals within limits. It is hardy to both drought and frost, and if permitted, may reach a height of 30 feet (9 m) with a spread of 10 feet (3 m). During spring, the cruel-looking, deciduous branches are softened by a profusion of clusters of scented, white blossoms. Dark green, glossy leaves soon put in an appearance, and during autumn, the show ends with a grand finale of striking, rounded, red berries. ✿ **PLANTING** A sunny situation is preferable but light shade can also be tolerated. The soil may be acid or alkaline, dry or wet, but should be cultivated well prior to planting. Young trees should be planted from autumn through to spring and kept free of weeds. To create a sturdy hedge, space plants 5 feet (1.5 m) apart. Watch for fireblight. ✿ **FLOWERING** Flowers from late spring to early summer, followed by attractive, red berries. ✿ **CULTIVATION** Prune hard if necessary during winter or early spring and remove suckers that rise from the roots annually. ✿ **PROPAGATION** From seed in autumn.

Davidia involucrata

Handkerchief tree ○ ◑ ❖❖❖

❀ **OTHER NAME** Dove tree, Ghost tree ❀ **DESCRIPTION** Few could forget the evocative white bracts of the shapely and rounded handkerchief tree, which dance in the gentlest of breezes. The flowers themselves are small, ball-shaped and virtually concealed by the attractive, drooping bracts. During autumn, they are replaced by inedible, pear-like fruits. Heart-shaped, bright green leaves with felted undersides are also a feature of this deciduous tree, which may eventually reach a height of 20 to 40 feet (6 to 12 m). Handkerchief trees will not flower until well established, and even then, are not guaranteed to put on a show every year thereafter. ❀ **PLANTING** Plant from autumn through to spring in a sunny or semi-shaded, protected position. The soil should be moist and well drained for optimum results, and poorer soils need to be enriched with organic matter. Allow plenty of room for the tree to grow.
❀ **FLOWERING** Blossoms appear during late spring or early summer and last for approximately two weeks. These are followed by green fruits in autumn. ❀ **CULTIVATION** Water generously during dry weather and mulch soil to prevent moisture loss. Prune to shape in winter during the tree's formative years. ❀ **PROPAGATION** By softwood cuttings taken during summer, or by sowing ripened seed during spring.

Erica arborea

Tree heath ○ pH ❖❖

❀ **DESCRIPTION** A close relative of the heathers, the tree heath is a shrubby, evergreen tree that may reach an eventual height of 20 feet (6 m) under ideal conditions, with a spread of up to 10 feet (3 m). Its bright green leaves are needle-shaped and occur in whorls along the branches. From late winter to spring, the tree heath becomes endowed with attractive, white, bell-shaped, fragrant flowers that occur in long clusters. For maximum effect, grow amongst other *Erica* species, *Callunas*, and other acid-loving plants. ❀ **PLANTING** At any time of year, plant into rich, well-drained, acid soil in an open, sunny position. Protection from frost is not necessary. Prior to planting, mix a good quantity of blood and bone and peat moss into the soil. ❀ **FLOWERING** A profusion of long-lasting flowers appear from late winter through to the end of spring. ❀ **CULTIVATION** Keep moist throughout the growing season, feed during spring, and mulch annually with peat moss or leaf litter. Prune hard after flowering if the tree heath outgrows its allotted space or needs reshaping. Otherwise, the removal of spent flower stems is all that is required. Avoid cultivating around the shallow roots and never apply lime. ❀ **PROPAGATION** Sow seed in spring.

Hippophae rhamnoides
Sea buckthorn ○ ❖❖❖

✿ **DESCRIPTION** An outstanding ornamental tree, grown for its attractive foliage, showy berries, and usefulness as a hedging plant. The sea buckthorn is deciduous with bushy, arching, and scaly branches. It often develops multiple trunks. In favourable conditions, it may reach a height of 25 feet (7.5 m). The slender leaves are silvery in appearance, and during spring, tiny, yellow flowers appear that are of little value ornamentally. In the presence of a male plant, the female produces attractive, long-lasting, bright orange berries during autumn. Birds are not attracted to these, however, due to their acidity. ✿ **PLANTING** Sea buckthorns grow particularly well in sandy, coastal areas and thrive in exposed, windy conditions. Plant between autumn and spring in a sunny position with light, well-drained soil. Poor, dry soils can also be tolerated. Grow one male plant for every six females to ensure a display of berries in autumn. ✿ **FLOWERING** Flowers appear mid-spring, followed by striking orange berries that provide colour until the end of winter. ✿ **CULTIVATION** Occasional, deep waterings throughout summer and a light application of complete fertilizer during spring is beneficial. Prune after flowering only if necessary. ✿ **PROPAGATION** Take softwood cuttings during summer, or sow seed during autumn.

Ilex aquifolium
English holly ○ ◐ pH ❖❖❖

✿ **OTHER NAME** Common holly ✿ **DESCRIPTION** A stately, evergreen tree with spreading branches that reaches a height of 50 feet (15 m) at maturity, with a spread of 14 feet (4.2 m). The leaves are thick, glossy, and dark green, and have sharp, wavy edges. During spring, small, white flowers appear in the leaf axils, followed by a mass of bright red berries during winter on pollinated female plants. The colourful berries and contrasting foliage make timely Christmas decorations for those living in the northern hemisphere. ✿ **PLANTING** Choose a sunny, protected position with moist, well-drained, neutral to acid soil. Gravelly and sandy loams are also suitable. Plant one male tree for every three females at a distance no greater than 100 feet (30 m) during late spring or early autumn. English hollies resent being transplanted, so it is advisable to set them out in the garden when young. ✿ **FLOWERING** During spring, followed by attractive red berries on female trees. ✿ **CULTIVATION** Keep moist throughout summer and drier during autumn and winter. English hollies can be pruned in late spring and respond well to pollarding. Main pests include the holly leaf miner and the holly aphid. ✿ **PROPAGATION** By seed in spring, or by cuttings taken from late summer to early winter.

Juniperus communis 'Compressa'
Dwarf juniper ○ pH ❖❖❖

❀ **DESCRIPTION** This small growing juniper is a popular landscaping
conifer, as it provides year-round colour and has a particularly attractive, conical
shape. Ideal for rockery and alpine gardens, it grows to 2 feet (6 cm) in
height. The juvenile foliage is prickly and yellow-green, while the upper,
mature growth is scale-like and golden. This two-toned effect is quite
unique to the conifer family. Other features of this ornamental evergreen tree
are the fleshy, globular fruits that develop in summer, and the abundant,
yellow cones that follow. The aromatic, golden foliage is heightened when
grown alongside plants with dark green leaves. ❀ **PLANTING** Plant
during autumn in an open, sunny position with deep, moist, and well-
drained soil. ❀ **FLOWERING** Flowers are not produced, however, berries
appear during summer followed by a mass of decorative cones.
❀ **CULTIVATION** Mulch the surrounding soil in order to prevent the
tree from drying out. Pruning is not necessary. ❀ **PROPAGATION** The
seed remains viable for a long period of time and should be sown in spring.
Cuttings will also strike readily with the assistance of bottom heat.

Larix kaempferi

Japanese larch ○ ❖❖❖

✿ **DESCRIPTION** This tree is one of the few fast-growing conifers, and is a valuable addition to any cool climate garden. The Japanese larch is a very vigorous grower once established, and its deciduous nature also separates it from many other conifers. Left unpruned, it develops a columnar shape and may reach a stately height of 100 feet (30 m), spreading to 20 feet (6 m). New shoots have a purplish appearance and are surrounded by clusters of flattened, needle-like leaves that may be either grey-green or bluish in hue. During autumn, the leaves develop attractive gold and russet tones before falling, to reveal the small, decorative, rose-like cones. ✿ **PLANTING** Larches do not enjoy wet feet but will grow happily in a sunny position in most soil types, provided it is deep and drains freely. In their homeland, Japanese larches thrive on mountain slopes and have developed the ability to withstand exposed, windy conditions. Plant trees when young during early spring or late autumn. ✿ **FLOWERING** Inconspicuous male and female flowers are produced during summer, followed by small, decorative cones. ✿ **CULTIVATION** Keep moist throughout the growing season. The leaves that fall each year will provide a moisture-retaining mulch. Generally, no pruning is required, but double leaders should be reduced to the strongest one. Older trees may have the lower, straggly branches removed. ✿ **PROPAGATION** By stratified seed sown in spring.

Magnolia x *soulangeana*

Chinese magnolia ○ pH ❖❖❖

❀ **OTHER NAME** Saucer magnolia ❀ **DESCRIPTION** *Magnolia* x *soulangeana* is undoubtedly the most popular of all the deciduous *Magnolia* species. It is a slow grower, but given the right conditions it will grow to 23 feet (7 m) with a spread of 10 feet (3 m). From late winter to early spring, the bare branches become clothed with brown, fuzzy flower buds, and from mid-spring, they open to reveal large, sweetly scented, white, cup-shaped blooms tinged with pink or red. As the flowers fade, the smooth, oval, green leaves emerge and provide dappled summer shade. Smooth, grey bark also adds to the appeal of this highly ornamental specimen tree. ❀ **PLANTING** Site the *Magnolia* in a prominent position where it can be fully appreciated from the house or street. Fertile, humus-rich soil is preferable with a neutral to acid pH, although a range of soil types can be tolerated. Plant during spring in a position with full sun and protection from strong winds. ❀ **FLOWERING** Flowers from mid-spring to early summer. ❀ **CULTIVATION** Mulch well and water deeply throughout the growing season. Pruning should be kept to a minimum, but when necessary, trim immediately after flowering. Dress annually with a mixture of compost and well-rotted animal manure. ❀ **PROPAGATION** By semi-ripe cuttings taken in summer.

Mespilus germanica

Medlar ○ ◑ ❖❖❖

✿ **DESCRIPTION** The medlar is commonly grown in cooler regions as a shade tree and is admired for its decorative flowers and fruits. It is a deciduous tree, sometimes spiny, growing to a height of 20 to 25 feet (6 to 7.5 m) with a wide-spreading crown. With age, it develops an attractive, twisted appearance. During autumn, the dark green, apple-like leaves turn a rich orange-brown before falling. White or pinkish singular flowers develop from spring to early summer. In frosty areas, the flowers are followed by brown, fuzzy fruits about the size of a golf ball. The fruits are edible but are only fit for consumption when they begin to rot. ✿ **PLANTING** The medlar thrives in full sun or light shade and prefers deep, moist, clay-based loams with good drainage. Plant during winter whilst dormant. ✿ **FLOWERING** Flowers appear from mid-spring to early summer depending on the climate. These are followed by small, rounded fruits in autumn, which cling to the tree well into winter. ✿ **CULTIVATION** The medlar is easy to grow, is relatively pest and disease resistant, and requires very little maintenance overall. Keep moist throughout summer and trim to shape during winter if required. Feed in spring with a complete fertilizer. ✿ **PROPAGATION** By seed, cuttings, or grafting.

Metasequoia glyptostroboides
Dawn redwood ○ ❖❖❖

❀ **OTHER NAME** Waterfir ❀ **DESCRIPTION** Once thought to be extinct, the dawn redwood was rediscovered in China in 1941 and has since become a popular garden conifer worldwide. It is a fast-growing, deciduous tree with upward-facing branches and an attractive, pyramidal shape. In its natural habitat, the dawn redwood grows to 120 feet (36 m). Cultivated specimens, however, are likely to reach 50 feet (15 m) at maturity, with a basal spread of 15 feet (4.5 m). The green foliage is soft and feathery in appearance, and during autumn, it turns a golden, bronze, or pinkish hue. Winter sees the textured, reddish bark revealed and the appearance of numerous, small, angular cones. ❀ **PLANTING** Choose a sunny, open position with ample room for the tree to grow. The soil should be fertile, moist, and well drained for optimum results, however, poorer soils can be tolerated. Work the soil well and plant any time from late autumn to early spring. ❀ **FLOWERING** Decorative cones develop during autumn and remain on the tree throughout winter. ❀ **CULTIVATION** Ensure the tree is well watered throughout the year, and feed annually in spring with a complete fertilizer. Pruning is not necessary unless a leading branch has been frost damaged. ❀ **PROPAGATION** By seed or cuttings taken in autumn.

Parrotia persica

Parrotia ○ pH ❖❖❖

❀ **OTHER NAME** Persian witch hazel, Ironwood, Irontree

❀ **DESCRIPTION** The parrotia is more akin to a shrub than a tree, due to its stout trunk and small size of 20 feet (6 m). It often develops a rather untidy shape but more than makes up for it with its incredibly handsome autumn foliage. In early spring, the bare winter branches develop clusters of small, brown bracts with protruding red stamens. These are promptly followed by brown seed capsules and attractive, rich green, oval, quilted leaves with scalloped margins. As winter approaches, they develop memorable yellow, orange, and crimson shades before falling. When dormant, the characteristic, flaky bark reveals the smooth, grey and white-blotched undersurface. Although lime tolerant, the tree colours best in acidic soils. ❀ **PLANTING** Plant any time between late autumn and early spring into moist, fertile, well-drained soil. For optimum results, choose a sunny or lightly shaded position with a soil pH of about 6.0 to 6.5. ❀ **FLOWERING** Petal-less flowers appear in early spring followed by the seed capsules. ❀ **CULTIVATION** If desired, remove the lower branches in winter to reveal the decorative bark, and lightly trim the entire tree for a bushier appearance. Dress annually with well-rotted compost and manure. ❀ **PROPAGATION** Sow seed early in spring or autumn.

Paulownia tomentosa
Paulownia ○ ❖❖❖

❧ **OTHER NAME** Royal paulownia ❧ **DESCRIPTION** The paulownia is capable of making astounding growth, is seldom troubled by pests, and is also resilient to pollution and seaside conditions. It is a deciduous tree reaching 30 to 40 feet (9 to 12 m) in height and bears large, heart-shaped, tomentose leaves. Once established, spikes of large, fragrant, trumpet-shaped, pale violet flowers develop in spring that are reminiscent of foxglove blooms. Although paulownias are hardy, occasionally the emerging buds are damaged by frost. After flowering, pointed, dry seed pods develop, which last throughout winter. ❧ **PLANTING** Choose a sunny, sheltered position away from cold winds, and plant during frost-free weather from late autumn to early spring. The soil needs to be deep, moist, and well drained with plenty of added organic matter. When purchasing a paulownia, be mindful that smaller specimens establish faster than advanced ones. Paulownias drop a fair amount of debris so avoid planting them near driveways or footpaths. ❧ **FLOWERING** Flowers appear in spring before new leaves emerge, followed in autumn by brown seed capsules. ❧ **CULTIVATION** Water deeply in the warmer months and feed twice-yearly with a complete fertilizer. Pruning is not necessary except to remove frost-damaged growth. ❧ **PROPAGATION** By seed.

Photinia villosa
Photinia ○ ◑ pH̬ ❖❖❖

✿ **DESCRIPTION** *Photinia villosa* is an ideal tree for the small home garden, growing to a conservative 20 feet (6 m) at most with an equal spread, giving it a rounded, shrub-like appearance. Unlike many other commonly grown *Photinia* species, *Photinia villosa* is deciduous and is prized for its stunning autumn foliage. The dark green adult leaves are oval in shape, downy on the underside, and have finely serrated edges. The juvenile leaves emerge with attractive bronze margins. During late spring, flattened clusters of white flowers emerge, contrasting beautifully with the leaves. Decorative, ovoid, red berries soon follow to extend the cheerful tonal parade. Autumn, however, is the time when *Photinia villosa* makes its proudest statement, producing leaves in bold shades of yellow, orange, and scarlet. ✿ **PLANTING** Planting is best carried out between late autumn and early spring. The site may be sunny or partially shaded, but *Photinia villosa* prefers free-draining, fertile, acid loam. Supplement poorer soils at planting time with generous quantities of compost and animal manure.
✿ **CULTIVATION** Keep moist throughout summer and feed during spring. Pruning is not normally required except to thin out old or dead wood. ✿ **PROPAGATION** By seed sown in autumn, or semi-hardwood cuttings in summer.

Quercus robur
English oak ○ p̂H ❖❖❖

❀ **DESCRIPTION** There are over 450 species of oaks worldwide, but the English variety is undoubtedly one of the most widely cultivated. The English oak is a stately, spreading tree, often used in street plantings, parks, and large gardens. Being slow-growing, one can expect it to reach 15 feet (4.5 m) high and 10 feet (3 m) wide within 20 years. Eventually, however, it will grow to three times this size with the aged branches becoming attractively gnarled. The dark, glossy leaves of the English oak are broad with wavy margins, changing hue in autumn. During summer, long catkins develop, followed by the brown, egg-shaped acorns that we have come to know so well. ❀ **PLANTING** The English oak prefers a sunny position with well-drained, alkaline soil. Plant during winter while the tree is dormant. Avoid planting in areas where the falling acorns and leaves are likely to cause problems. ❀ **FLOWERING** Catkins appear from late spring to early summer followed by a mass of acorns. ❀ **CULTIVATION** Prune during winter or early spring if necessary, removing any damaged or unwanted branches. Watch for invasions of the oak-leaf miner in autumn. ❀ **PROPAGATION** By seed.

Rhus typhina
Staghorn sumac ○ ◑ ❖❖❖

❀ **OTHER NAMES** Velvet sumac, Virginian sumac

❀ **DESCRIPTION** Despite the Rhus's notorious reputation for causing severe skin allergies in some people, the staghorn sumac is a useful specimen tree for the home garden. It is a rapid grower and produces one of the most breathtaking autumn displays of all deciduous trees. At maturity, the staghorn sumac reaches a height of 25 feet (7.6 m), spreading broadly. When young, the branches, shoots, and leaves are covered in fine, red hairs, and during summer, panicles of tiny, yellowish flowers emerge. If pollinated, the female flowers produce decorative clusters of red berries.

❀ **PLANTING** The staghorn sumac will tolerate a wide range of soils and positions. It is hardy to pollution and frost but does not like to dry out. If the soil is sandy or gravelly, incorporate generous amounts of compost at planting time to aid water retention. ❀ **FLOWERING** Inconspicuous flowers appear from mid to late summer followed by rounded, hairy fruits in autumn. ❀ **CULTIVATION** Prune only to remove dead or damaged branches or to improve upon the tree's natural shape. Do this during winter while the tree is dormant and be sure to wear protective clothing.

❀ **PROPAGATION** By semi-hardwood cuttings in summer, root cuttings during winter, or by seed in autumn.

Sophora japonica
Japanese pagoda tree ○ ❖❖❖

❀ **OTHER NAME** Chinese scholar tree ❀ **DESCRIPTION** The
Japanese pagoda tree has long been in cultivation and is still the most popular
form of *Sophora* grown today. It is a deciduous, spreading tree with an ability
to grow to 40 feet (12 m), however, it is often pruned to more conservative
heights. Notable features of the Japanese pagoda include dark green, fern-
like leaves and prolific sprays of creamy-white, pea-shaped flowers that appear
during summer when the tree is over 20 years of age. Masses of yellow-green
pods follow in autumn. ❀ **PLANTING** Japanese pagodas grow in all but
the coldest of areas and will adapt to a wide range of soils. For best results,
choose a sunny area with deep, moist, well-drained soil and plant from winter
to early spring. ❀ **FLOWERING** Flowers appear in profusion during late
summer and last for one month. The seed pods cling to the tree well into
winter. ❀ **CULTIVATION** Water deeply during spring and summer and
mulch generously. The Japanese pagoda tends to produce low-growing
branches, so remove them if necessary during autumn to provide sufficient
head room. Apical branches can also be trimmed back to reduce the overall
height. Pests and diseases are rarely a problem. ❀ **PROPAGATION** Seed
readily germinates when sown in autumn.

Sorbus aucuparia

Rowan ○ ◑ ❖❖❖

✿ **OTHER NAME** Mountain ash ✿ **DESCRIPTION** The rowan tree
is a familiar garden treasure, with its handsome, grey-green foliage and
decorative berries. It is deciduous and grows to 35 feet (10.5 m), spreading
up to 15 feet (4.5 m) at maturity. During spring, clusters of white flowers
appear, which are followed by masses of orangy-red berries that birds find
irresistible. Autumn-time sees the leaves transform into vivid shades of
yellow and orange before they fall. The rowan tree is normally grown as a
lawn specimen and thrives in cool climate gardens. It is hardy to frost, strong
winds, salt spray, and city pollution. ✿ **PLANTING** Plant during winter
when the tree is dormant into a position receiving full sun or light shade.
Most soils can be tolerated, so long as they are well drained and moisture
retentive. Poorer soils can be enriched at planting time with compost and
manure. ✿ **FLOWERING** Flowers from early spring, followed in summer
by attractive clusters of rounded berries. ✿ **CULTIVATION** During late
winter, prune young specimens to encourage branching. Older trees do not
normally require pruning except to remove damaged or unwanted branches.
The rowan tree is susceptible to fireblight. ✿ **PROPAGATION** By
softwood cuttings in summer, or by seed in autumn.

Stewartia pseudocamellia (syn. *Stuartia*)

Stewartia ○ pH ❖❖❖

❀ **OTHER NAMES** Japanese stewartia, False camellia

❀ **DESCRIPTION** *Stewartia pseudocamellia* makes a decorative addition
to the sunny shrub border. It is a deciduous tree with a spreading crown and
is relatively slow-growing. Eventually, it will reach a height of 25 feet (7.6 m)
with a spread of 15 feet (4.5 m). The species name relates to the white
camellia-like flowers with yellow centres, which appear throughout summer.
Its handsome, oval, mid-green leaves turn red and yellow in autumn. As the
tree matures, the bark develops a flaky appearance, which adds character.

❀ **PLANTING** The Stewartia grows happily in all but the coldest of areas
and requires a sunny position with protection from strong winds. The roots,
however, need to be shaded from the sun, and the soil should be fertile, moist,
and well drained, with a neutral to acid pH. Plant the Stewartia when young,
during late winter or early spring. ❀ **FLOWERING** Flowers appear from
early to midsummer, depending on the climate. Each bloom lasts for only a
few days, but they open in succession over a period of several weeks.

❀ **CULTIVATION** Dress annually with organic matter and keep well
mulched. Pruning is rarely necessary, and the Stewartia resents being
transplanted once established. ❀ **PROPAGATION** By seed in autumn,
or by softwood cuttings taken during summer.

Styrax japonicus

Snowbell ○ ◑ pH ❖❖❖

✿ **OTHER NAMES** Silverballs, Storax ✿ **DESCRIPTION** *Styrax japonicus* is a superb ornamental tree due to its small size of 15 to 20 feet (4.5 to 6 m) with an equal spread, and its beautifully combined flower and foliage display. It is slow growing and deciduous in habit and is best planted where the flowers can be observed from underneath, such as on a bank or near a patio. In spring, glossy, dark green leaves emerge, followed by pendular sprays of fragrant, bell-shaped, white flowers with contrasting yellow stamens. During autumn, the leaves develop attractive red and yellow tones, and inedible, grey fruits appear, which remain until winter. ✿ **PLANTING** Plant from autumn to early spring in a sunny or partially shaded position. The soil needs to be slightly acidic, moist, and well drained for optimum results. Impoverished soils should be enriched with compost at planting time. ✿ **FLOWERING** Flowers from early to midsummer.
✿ **CULTIVATION** The snowbell does not like dry conditions, so mulch well to preserve soil moisture and water regularly throughout summer. Feed each spring with compost and well-rotted manure and prune young specimens during winter. An established snowbell seldom requires pruning and is relatively pest free. ✿ **PROPAGATION** Multiply by sowing seed in autumn, or by taking softwood cuttings in summer.

Taxus baccata
Yew ○ p̂H ❖❖❖

❀ **OTHER NAME** English yew ❀ **DESCRIPTION** The English yew
has been cultivated for centuries and is used extensively for hedging and
topiary work. It is painfully slow growing but long lived, with a yearly
growth of around 8 inches (20 cm). Left untrimmed, it can be expected to
reach a height of 33 feet (10 m) after 60 years, with an equal spread. The
English yew is evergreen with dark green, flattened, needle-shaped leaves
arranged in whorls around the stem. Male flowers are inconspicuous and
produce inordinate amounts of pollen. Female trees produce green globules,
which when fertilized, develop highly-decorative, red fruits, botanically
known as 'arils'. All parts of the tree are poisonous apart from the red, fleshy
aril. ❀ **PLANTING** Plant during autumn in a sunny position with moist,
well-drained, alkaline soil. The English yew can tolerate both drought and
frost, and flourish in a wide variety of climates. ❀ **FLOWERING** Male
trees bear tiny, pollen-bearing flowers in late winter. Once pollinated, female
trees develop red, fleshy fruits in autumn. ❀ **CULTIVATION** Hedging
specimens should be trimmed annually in autumn, otherwise pruning is not
generally required. Feed in spring with a complete fertilizer and lime if
necessary. ❀ **PROPAGATION** By seed sown in autumn, or by heeled
cuttings taken from late summer to winter.

Tilia cordata
Small-leaved lime ○ ◑ ❖❖❖

✿ **OTHER NAMES** Small-leaved linden, Littleleaf linden

✿ **DESCRIPTION** The lime tree is best known for its ability to attract bees and for the resultant wild lime honey that they produce. The small-leaved lime is a fast grower, reaching an eventual height of 50 feet (15 m) and spreading 35 feet (10.5 m), and is normally planted as a shade tree in parks, large gardens, and along roadsides. Its heart-shaped leaves are glossy and green above, with bluish-green undersides. In cool climates, the leaves turn yellow in autumn before falling. The blackish trunk is cracked in appearance and suckers freely. ✿ **PLANTING** The small-leaved lime does well in full sun or semi-shade and prefers soils that are moist, deep, and well drained. Plant during winter or early spring. ✿ **FLOWERING** From mid-summer, the small-leaved lime is festooned with masses of tiny, yellowish blossoms, followed in autumn by small, green, inedible fruits which cling until winter. ✿ **CULTIVATION** Grows best in cool climate gardens and should be kept moist throughout summer. Young specimens respond well to pruning in winter and are easily trained as espaliers. Established specimen trees rarely require pruning. Remove suckers as required.

✿ **PROPAGATION** Propagate by seed, layers, or cuttings taken in summer.

Ulmus parvifolia
Chinese elm ○ ❖❖❖

✿ **OTHER NAME** Lacebark ✿ **DESCRIPTION** An outstanding
deciduous shade tree that is only suitable for large gardens or parkland where
it has sufficient space to spread and grow to its full height of 50 feet (15 m),
this handsome tree has a spreading shape and a rounded top. The older bark
is mottled and patchy, and the foliage is small, oval, and glossy green, turning
red in late autumn. It holds its foliage for longer than many other deciduous
trees, however, the small flowers do not bloom until autumn, unlike most
elms, which flower before the foliage in early spring. The variety 'Pendens'
remains evergreen in warm to hot climates. ✿ **PLANTING** Choose an
open, sunny position with plenty of space for rapid growth. The soils should
be deep, well drained, and fertile, and the young tree should be watered
well during the first few summers if conditions are hot and dry.
✿ **FLOWERING** Inconspicuous flowers and attractive red foliage appear
in autumn. ✿ **CULTIVATION** Once established, the Chinese elm will
require very little attention, however, watch for Dutch Elm disease, which
can be fatal. ✿ **PROPAGATION** Can be grown from seed or suckers in
autumn, or propagated by softwood cuttings in summer.

Aronia arbutifolia

Red chokeberry ○ ◑ ❖❖❖

❀ **DESCRIPTION** An easy-to-cultivate deciduous shrub that makes upright growth during the first few years, then develops a graceful, arching habit as the plant matures. Growing to 9 feet (2.7 m) in the right situation, this shrub requires little attention once established. It is valued for its foliage, flowers, and fruit, making it an attractive feature for most of the year. The foliage is dark green, changing to a rich red in autumn. The small white flowers with red anthers are prolific, followed by decorative red berries that give the plant its common name. ❀ **PLANTING** Adaptable to most soils and conditions, the chokeberry will do well if planted either in full sun or semi-shade in any moderately rich garden soil with good drainage. If situated in full sun the plant will give a more dramatic autumn foliage display.

❀ **FLOWERING** The flowers bloom in spring, followed by the berries in early summer. ❀ **CULTIVATION** Little care is required once plants are established. Mulch around the base of the shrub to reduce the need for watering in summer. Prune lightly if required. ❀ **PROPAGATION** By softwood or semi-ripe cuttings in summer, or by division in autumn or spring.

Aucuba japonica 'Variegata'
Gold dust plant ◗ ● ❖❖

✿ **OTHER NAMES** Japanese laurel, spotted laurel
✿ **DESCRIPTION** A handsome evergreen shrub native to Japan, grown
for its large, dramatic leaves. Growing to a height of 10 feet (3 m), the gold
dust plant has a pleasant, rounded shape and is well covered with large, glossy
deep green leaves that are speckled with golden yellow markings. Aucubas
have both male and female plants, which can be grown near to each other
so that the female plants will produce decorative bright red berries which
are followed by small, star-shaped, purple flowers. In cold climates it can
be grown successfully as a house plant in a large container, placed in a cool,
shaded position. ✿ **PLANTING** Easy to cultivate in a wide range of soils,
providing conditions are not waterlogged. Choose a dappled, sheltered
situation that is protected from strong sun in midsummer, which can burn
the foliage. ✿ **FLOWERING** The small flowers appear in mid-spring,
followed by decorative red fruits on the female plants. ✿ **CULTIVATION**
If the shrub is growing too large for its position it can be easily brought into
shape by a hard pruning of the old shoots in spring. Water well during hot
or dry weather, however, take care not to overwater, especially if drainage is
not excellent. ✿ **PROPAGATION** Easy to propagate from semi-ripe
cuttings taken in summer.

Berberis thunbergii 'Atropurpuria'
Japanese barberry ○ ◑ ❖❖❖

✿ **DESCRIPTION** A graceful, arching, deciduous shrub that is prized for its foliage, which brings a touch of red to the garden. The Japanese barberry is a thorny plant, growing to 7 feet (2 m), with an open habit and stems covered with reddish leaves throughout the entire growing season. The small, yellow flowers are tinged with red and make a wonderful contrast against the red hues of the foliage. Following the flowers are small decorative berries that are egg-shaped and bright red. Barberries make excellent thorny hedges, or can be used as a feature plant in a mixed shrub border. ✿ **PLANTING** An adaptable plant for a sunny or semi-shaded situation. Any reasonably good garden soil is adequate for successful cultivation, providing conditions are not waterlogged. Incorporate some well-rotted organic matter or compost at planting time, and mulch to maintain soil moisture until the plant is established. ✿ **FLOWERING** The small flowers bloom in spring, followed immediately by a crop of small, showy berries.

✿ **CULTIVATION** Once established, little care or attention will be required. Prune back stems if they overhang paths or walkways, as the thorns can be a problem. ✿ **PROPAGATION** By softwood or semi-ripe cuttings taken in summer.

Buxus sempervirens
Common box ○ ◐ ❖❖❖

✿ **DESCRIPTION** A useful and hardy evergreen shrub that is excellent for hedging, edging, creating borders, or topiary. Native to southern Europe, the common box grows to a height of 18 feet (5.4 m) unless trimmed, and is very long-lived, which makes it ideal as a permanent feature in the formal garden. The deep green foliage is small, oblong, and glossy and there are several worthwhile varieties, including 'Albo-marginata', which has green and white margined leaves, and 'Suffruticosa', a dwarf form with mid-green leaves that is frequently used as an edging plant. The flowers are insignificant.
✿ **PLANTING** A durable plant that will thrive in most soils, except where bad drainage creates boggy, waterlogged conditions. Choose a sunny or semi-shaded situation and add some organic matter to the soil to boost the plant's growth. ✿ **FLOWERING** The flowers are small and insignificant.
✿ **CULTIVATION** When grown as a hedge, box will need trimming during summer, the main growing period. Encourage vigorous new growth by cutting back stems to 30 cm or less in late spring. Mulch between plants to prevent weed growth. ✿ **PROPAGATION** Semi-ripe cuttings can be taken in summer.

Callicarpa dichotoma
Beauty berry ○ ◑ ❖❖❖

✿ **OTHER NAME** Jewel berry ✿ **DESCRIPTION** A most attractive, deciduous, erect shrub with arching branches that give it an elegant outline. Native to China and Korea, this plant has showy violet to metallic purple berries that remain on the branches after the foliage has turned yellow and fallen. It is these berries that make the plant outstanding, as the flowers are pale pink and rather inconspicuous. The beauty berry can grow to 4 feet (1.2 m) at maturity, and is a good feature plant in a mixed shrub border or at the back of a flowerbed. In spring, it is clothed with masses of pointed, finely toothed leaves that are spotted on the undersides. ✿ **PLANTING** Choose a sunny, open position, or one that is slightly shaded, and ensure that the soil is moderately rich and well-drained. The beauty berry can withstand a certain degree of cold in winter, however, it is not really suited to areas with heavy frost or snow. ✿ **FLOWERING** The dramatic berries create a wonderful display in late autumn, after the foliage has fallen from the stems. The small, summer flowers are inconspicuous. ✿ **CULTIVATION** Little general maintenance is necessary once the plant is well established. If pruning, take care not to disturb the pleasant, arching shape. ✿ **PROPAGATION** Softwood cuttings can be taken in summer.

Calluna vulgaris

Heather ○ pH ❖❖❖

✿ **OTHER NAMES** Ling, Broom, Scotch heather

✿ **DESCRIPTION** A worthwhile evergreen plant that is easy to grow if the correct soil conditions are provided. Not to be confused with heath (*Erica carnea*), which has a similar appearance. Growing to 18 inches (45 cm) in height, the plant has a full, bushy shape and stems of slightly fleshy foliage that varies in colour from bright green to yellow, orange, and red according to the variety. The small, bell-shaped flowers also vary considerably in colour. Attractive cultivars include 'County Wicklow', which has double, shell-pink flowers; 'Elegantissima', which has sprays of lilac flowers; and 'Darkness', which has deep crimson blooms. ✿ **PLANTING** Heather does best on poor soils that are slightly acid—over-rich soil causes rapid stem and foliage growth, and eventually the plant will die. Soil should be moisture retentive but never too moist, as it resents poor drainage. Full sun produces the best flowering. ✿ **FLOWERING** Flowers appear over several months from midsummer to late autumn. ✿ **CULTIVATION** In cool to cold climates, mulch around the plant with straw during winter to prevent the ground from getting too cold. Otherwise little care is necessary when the plant is established. ✿ **PROPAGATION** Softwood cuttings can be taken in late summer.

Camellia japonica
Camellia ◑ pH ❖❖

❀ **DESCRIPTION** One of the most highly prized of all garden shrubs, the camellia is very easy to cultivate if the correct soil conditions are provided. Plants vary considerably within the japonica group, with many growing to an extremely large size, up to 45 feet (13.6 m) at maturity. In general, camellias are large shrubs with a good covering of deep green, glossy foliage and a showy display of waxy flowers that can be single, semi-double, or double in a variety of colours, including white, pink, red, or variegated forms. ❀ **PLANTING** Camellias will thrive in moderately rich, moist, and slightly acid soil in a semi-shaded situation. Afternoon sun is preferable to morning sun, especially for the pale pink or white flowered varieties, which will get scorched petals. Water well until plants are established. ❀ **FLOWERING** Varies according to the variety, but generally, from late winter to early summer. ❀ **CULTIVATION** Like all shallow-rooted plants, camellias like a good layer of leaf mulch to prevent the soil surface from drying out. Feed annually, when flower buds are forming or immediately after flowering, with a specially formulated camellia fertilizer. Aphids, thrips, and scale insects may cause a problem. ❀ **PROPAGATION** From semi-ripe cuttings taken in summer, or from hardwood cuttings taken in winter.

Caragana arborescens

Pea tree ○ ◐ ❖❖❖

❀ **OTHER NAME** Siberian pea tree ❀ **DESCRIPTION** This is one of the hardiest and most easily cultivated shrubs available for home gardens. Native to Siberia and Manchuria, it seems capable of surviving even the most difficult conditions with a minimum of care. Growing to 18 feet (5.4 m), the Siberian pea tree is actually a shrub, which can be used most effectively as a screening plant or windbreak. It is a member of the pea family, and as such, has distinctive, bright yellow pea flowers that make an excellent display in summer. The form 'Pendula' has more graceful, arching branches and the same bright yellow pea flowers. ❀ **PLANTING** This vigorous shrub will grow in most soils and climates, in either full sun or partial shade. Reasonably good drainage is preferable, and staking during the first year of growth will help while it becomes established. ❀ **FLOWERING** Flowers over many weeks in summer. ❀ **CULTIVATION** Water well after planting, and keep water up to the plant during the first few summers if conditions are dry. Prune back after flowering if the branches become leggy. ❀ **PROPAGATION** Softwood cuttings can be taken summer, or from seed sown in spring.

Chaenomeles speciosa

Japanese quince ○ ❖❖❖

❧ **OTHER NAMES** Flowering quince, Japonica

❧ **DESCRIPTION** A highly prized, thorny, deciduous shrub that can be used for hedging, or as a colourful feature plant in any sunny part of the garden. Native to China, the flowering quince grows to 6 feet (1.8 m) with a rounded, spreading outline and slender stems that are covered with oval, glossy, deep green foliage. The bright red spring flowers are the main attraction of this plant, appearing on the stems prior to the foliage, then followed by large, greenish-yellow fruits. There are several worthwhile varieties, including 'Simonii', which has double red flowers, and 'Nivalis', which has single flowers of pure white. ❧ **PLANTING** Choose a sunny, open position and any moderately rich, well-drained soil. This shrub can be trained against a wall by cutting back the side shoots after flowering. ❧ **FLOWERING** Flowers in early spring. ❧ **CULTIVATION** Water well until the plant is established, and mulch to prevent weed growth around the base. Scale can be a problem in warmer climates. ❧ **PROPAGATION** By softwood cuttings taken in summer, or by seed collected in autumn. Cultivars will not reproduce from seed.

Choisya ternata
Mexican orange blossom ○ ❖❖

❀ **DESCRIPTION** A popular evergreen shrub that has fragrant foliage and flowers. Growing to 9 feet (2.7 m), Mexican orange blossom has a rounded, dense shape and a good covering of aromatic, bright green leaves all year round. The charming white flowers are small and star-like, appearing in clusters in spring and sometimes again in autumn. They have a strong, heady fragrance, especially when bathed in the warmth of the sun. It is an ideal plant for a sunny border, or for positioning near a gazebo or outdoor entertaining area where its fragrance can be properly enjoyed.
❀ **PLANTING** Plant in a sheltered, sunny position that is not exposed to strong winds or frosts in winter. The soil must be moderately rich and well-drained, preferably with some well-rotted organic matter added prior to planting. In cold climates it makes an excellent greenhouse plant if kept pruned. ❀ **FLOWERING** Recurrent flowering in spring and then again in autumn. ❀ **CULTIVATION** After planting mulch well with compost, and water in summer during the first season or two until the plant's roots are established. ❀ **PROPAGATION** Easy to propagate from semi-ripe cuttings taken in summer.

Corylopsis spicata

Corylopsis ◑ pH ✤✤✤

✿ **OTHER NAME** Spike winter hazel

✿ **DESCRIPTION** A pleasant deciduous shrub valued for its early spring flowers, which appear before the foliage. This early flowering habit brings a wonderful splash of colour to the garden. In cooler climates, however, the flower buds are sometimes destroyed by late frosts. Growing to 6 feet (1.8 m) in height, corylopsis has an open, spreading habit and pendulous racemes of delightful, fragrant yellow flowers that appear before the pale green, hazel-like foliage emerges. The flowers are followed by decorative woody fruits. ✿ **PLANTING** Select a sheltered, semi-shaded situation and prepare the soil well by adding plenty of leaf mould to create slightly acid, moist conditions. Mulch with leaves and water well, especially during summer, until the plant is well established. ✿ **FLOWERING** Flowers in early to mid-spring. ✿ **CULTIVATION** In cold areas, provide some shelter from late frosts, which may destroy the flower buds. The canopy of an overhanging evergreen tree may be sufficient. If pruning, take care not to destroy the attractive, natural shape of the shrub.

✿ **PROPAGATION** By taking softwood cuttings in summer, or by gathering and sowing seed in autumn.

Corynabutilon vitifolium (syn. *Abutilon vitifolium*)
Grape-leaved flowering maple ○ ❖

❀ **DESCRIPTION** A delightful and fast-growing upright, evergreen shrub that is ideal for any sunny, open part of the garden, or the back of a mixed flower bed or border. Growing to 14 feet (4 m) in height, it has a handsome shape and masses of lobed and sharply-toothed grey-green foliage. The flowers of this shrub make it an outstanding garden specimen. They are large, blue-purple and bowl-shaped. The variety 'Album' produces masses of large, wide-open white flowers over many weeks. ❀ **PLANTING** This shrub will not withstand very cold winters, and is only grown in warmer climates. It must have a sunny open position and the soil should be enriched with plenty of organic matter in the form of well rotted compost, prior to planting. Spring, when the soil has warmed, is the best time to establish the shrub, watering it well after planting and making sure the soil doesn't dry out in summer. Good drainage is important. ❀ **FLOWERING** The flowers appear in a profusion from late spring to early summer. ❀ **CULTIVATION** Keep the water up to the plant in summer if conditions are hot and dry. Mulch with leaves or bark to keep weeds from the base of the plant. Tip prune young plants to encourage a more bushy shape. ❀ **PROPAGATION** From semi-ripe cuttings taken in summer.

Cotoneaster horizontalis
Rock spray ○ ◐ ❖❖❖

✿ **OTHER NAME** Wall spray ✿ **DESCRIPTION** A tough and easy-
to-grow deciduous plant that makes an excellent ground-covering shrub, or
that can be espaliered against a wall for a most dramatic effect. This variety
of cotoneaster grows to 3 feet (1 m) in height, with a spreading, horizontal
branching habit that makes it useful for creating special features, such as low
hedges or ground covers. From spring it is covered with masses of glossy,
dark green foliage that changes to a soft red in late autumn. The pinkish-white
flowers are small, followed by a wonderful display of bright red berries along
the stems. The form 'Variegata' has foliage edged with white, and makes
an ideal plant for rockery gardens. ✿ **PLANTING** This plant is useful
because it can withstand quite dry soil conditions that cannot be tolerated
by many other species. Choose a sunny or semi-shaded position, and make
sure that the soil is well-drained, never waterlogged. ✿ **FLOWERING** The
small flowers bloom in summer, followed by red berries in autumn.
✿ **CULTIVATION** Mulch around plants, especially in the rockery
garden, to prevent perennial weed growth. ✿ **PROPAGATION** Easy to
propagate from semi-ripe cuttings taken in summer.

Elaeagnus pungens
Thorny elaeagnus ○ ◑ ❖❖

❀ **DESCRIPTION** An easy-to-grow and reliable evergreen shrub that can be used for hedging, or to provide a shelter belt planting in exposed or coastal gardens. Thorny elaeagnus grows to 12 feet (3.6 m) in height, and is covered with long, prickly branches that grow in a horizontal fashion. The foliage is oval-shaped with wavy margins, glossy dark green on the top and silvery underneath. The fragrant flowers are bell-shaped and silvery cream in colour. Varieties include 'Aurea', which has rich yellow leaf margins; 'Maculata', which has foliage blotched with yellow; and 'Tricolor', which has green, yellow, and pinkish-white variegated foliage. ❀ **PLANTING** Choose a sunny or semi-shaded position and ensure that the soil is moderately rich with good drainage. Heavy soils can be improved with the addition of plenty of well-rotted organic matter. ❀ **FLOWERING** The cream flowers bloom in autumn. ❀ **CULTIVATION** Water deeply during hot, dry spells in summer and mulch to help retain some soil moisture. If growing as a hedge, trimming should be done in late summer. ❀ **PROPAGATION** From seed in autumn, or semi-ripe cuttings taken in summer.

Erica cinerea
Bell heather ○ ◐ pH ❖❖❖

❀ **OTHER NAME** Twisted heath ❀ **DESCRIPTION** A compact, bushy evergreen shrub that grows to 1 feet (30 cm) in height. The secret with successfully growing Erica is to find exactly the right position and soil, because once established they will require very little maintenance. This species has a good covering of needle-like, mid-green leaves, changing to bronze in autumn, and masses of tiny, bell-shaped flowers that can be white, pink, or dark red according to the variety. Cultivars include 'Atrorubens', which has ruby-red flowers, 'Golden Drop', which has copper-coloured foliage and attractive pink flowers, and 'Springwood White', which is the most vigorous of the white-flowering types. ❀ **PLANTING** This plant will thrive if given a warm, dry position and acid soil that has been enriched with leaf mould. Good drainage is essential, and some protection and strong winds and rain will be beneficial. ❀ **FLOWERING** Flowers over many weeks, from early summer to early autumn. ❀ **CULTIVATION** Mulch with maple leaves to help create the right soil pH, and prune back quite hard after flowering to maintain a good shape. ❀ **PROPAGATION** From cuttings taken in summer.

Escallonia hybrids
Escallonia ○ ◐ ❖❖

❧ **DESCRIPTION** A group of very useful and sometimes quite vigorous evergreen shrubs that are frequently used as hedging plants or windbreaks in coastal or other exposed gardens. Growing to 5 feet (1.5 m) and spreading to create a pleasant, dense shape, escallonia has slender arching stems covered with handsome, glossy, mid-green foliage. The showy, fragrant flowers vary according to the hybrid. Hybrids include 'Apple Blossom', which has a profusion of pretty pink flowers, 'Donard Beauty', which has large, vivid rose-crimson flowers, and 'Iveyi', which has tubular, pure-white flowers.
❧ **PLANTING** This durable group of shrubs can withstand strong winds and exposed conditions, except in cool to cold climates where they are best planted near a sunny wall. The soil should be moderately rich and well-drained, with organic matter added to help retain soil moisture. ❧ **FLOWERING** Summer is the main flowering period. ❧ **CULTIVATION** Mulch around the base of the shrub to help prevent the soil from drying out after rain or watering. If grown as a hedge, trimming should be done after flowering in late summer or autumn. ❧ **PROPAGATION** From softwood cuttings taken in summer.

Euonymus japonicus
Evergreen spindle tree ○ ◑ ❖❖

❀ **OTHER NAME** Japanese spindle tree ❀ **DESCRIPTION** A densely foliated, evergreen shrub with an upright growing habit, reaching a height of 15 feet (4.5 m) at maturity. Often used as a hedge or windbreak, especially in windy, exposed gardens, the spindle tree has masses of attractive, glossy, deep green leaves and small, starry, greenish-white flowers that are followed by round, pink berries with orange seeds. Varieties include 'Albomarginatus', a much smaller-growing shrub with white margined leaves; 'Aureomarginatus', which is a popular, medium-growing shrub with yellow margined leaves; and 'Aureus', which has rounded leaves blotched with yellow in the centre. ❀ **PLANTING** Good drainage is important, although if grown in full sun organic matter must be added to the soil to ensure that it does not dry out too much in summer. Mulch after planting to help maintain soil moisture. ❀ **FLOWERING** Flowers appear in summer, followed by fruits. ❀ **CULTIVATION** The spindle tree can be trimmed in late summer to form a neat hedge. Watch for attack by caterpillars or mildew. ❀ **PROPAGATION** Easy to propagate by semi-ripe cuttings in summer, or from seed collected in autumn.

Mahonia japonica
Japanese mahonia ◑ ● ❖❖

✿ **DESCRIPTION** A useful, upright, evergreen shrub for a partially shaded part of the garden, with masses of deep green leaves that consist of many spiny leaflets. The flowers appear in long, spreading sprays and are very fragrant. They are a soft yellow colour, and are followed by attractive purple-blue fruits. Growing to 10 feet (3 m), the shrub has a pleasant rounded shape and makes a good specimen tree because of its attractive foliage, flowers, and fruit. The deeply fissured bark is also a valued feature of this plant.

✿ **PLANTING** An adaptable plant, the mahonia likes moderately rich and well-drained soils that are not too dry. Add organic matter at planting time, and mulch well to prevent the soil surface from drying out, especially during summer. A semi-shaded position is preferable. ✿ **FLOWERING** The flowers appear from late autumn to spring, followed by the decorative fruits.

✿ **CULTIVATION** During hot, dry weather deep-watering will encourage the downward growth of roots. ✿ **PROPAGATION** From semi-ripe cuttings taken in summer, or from seed collected in autumn.

Philadelphus x *lemoinei*

Mock orange ○ ◑ ❖❖❖

✿ **DESCRIPTION** One of the most attractive of the mock oranges, this hybrid is a cross between *Philadelphus microphyllus* and *Philadelphus coronarius*. It is a deciduous, upright shrub, growing to 6 feet (1.8 m), with slightly arching stems and masses of small oval to lance-shaped leaves that are mid-green in colour and slightly hairy on the undersides. It is the flowers that make this an outstanding plant. They are small, white and intensely fragrant, covering the entire shrub profusely over many weeks.

✿ **PLANTING** Choose an open, sunny position that has a degree of shade during summer if the climate is hot, as the flowers will suffer from heat exposure. The soil should be quite rich, with plenty of organic matter in the form of well-rotted manures or compost added to increase fertility. Good drainage is important. ✿ **FLOWERING** Flowers from early to midsummer. ✿ **CULTIVATION** Water deeply during hot weather, and mulch to prevent the soil surface from drying out. After flowering has finished, cut back the older shoots to encourage new flowering shoots for the following season. Protect from aphids, paying particular attention to the tender new growth. ✿ **PROPAGATION** From softwood cuttings taken in summer.

Pieris japonica
Pieris ◑ ● pH ❖❖❖

✿ **OTHER NAME** Japanese andromeda ✿ **DESCRIPTION** This shrub is quite fussy about soil conditions, but once established it will thrive with very little maintenance. Pieris is a handsome evergreen shrub that can grow to 9 feet (2.7 m) with an upright shape and very attractive foliage. The leaves are lustrous and deep green, however, the new foliage growth is a brilliant bronze and makes a dramatic display following the flowers. The flowers appear as dense sprays covered with urn-shaped, creamy white blooms that have a waxy finish. There are many varieties, including 'Christmas Cheer', which has delicate pink flowers and 'Variegata', which has variegated leaves with white margins. ✿ **PLANTING** Choose a semi-shaded position in preference to full shade if the spring foliage display is valued. The soil must be well-drained and acidic, but capable of holding moisture well. The addition of peat at planting time will help create an ideal growing environment. ✿ **FLOWERING** Flowers appear in spring, followed by bronze foliage tip-growth. ✿ **CULTIVATION** In cold climates the young foliage tips can be killed by frost in spring, so they should be trimmed off or given some protection. Mulch well with rotted leaf mould, and water deeply in dry summer conditions. ✿ **PROPAGATION** From semi-ripe cuttings, or soft-tip cuttings, taken in summer.

Potentilla fruticosa
Shrubby cinquefoil ○ ◑ ❖❖❖

✿ **OTHER NAMES** Golden hardback, Widdy, Fingerbush

✿ **DESCRIPTION** This excellent, woody shrub is native over all of the northern hemisphere, which is quite unusual. Reaching 4 feet (1.2 m) in height, it is a densely growing, spreading shrub that is prized for its hardiness and resistance to virtually all pests and diseases. The foliage is deep green and quite attractive, and the large, showy flowers are saucer-shaped and bright yellow in colour. Because of their ease of cultivation, the potentillas are wonderful plants for mixed flowerbeds or borders, where they will provide a solid outline as well as wonderful summer colour. ✿ **PLANTING** Choose an open, sunny position and enrich the soil with some well-rotted compost to help it retain moisture during summer. Good drainage is essential.

✿ **FLOWERING** The flowering period is extensive, from late spring until the end of summer. ✿ **CULTIVATION** Once established, very little care or maintenance will be required. Mulch to keep weeds from around the base of the plant, and water well if the shrub becomes stressed during hot, dry weather. ✿ **PROPAGATION** Softwood cuttings can be taken in summer, or raised from seed sown in autumn.

Rosa chinensis
China rose ○ ❖❖

❀ **OTHER NAME** Bengal rose ❀ **DESCRIPTION** A native of China, this durable species rose grows to 3 feet (1 m) with upright stems and a good covering of mid-green foliage. The flowers are classic, old-fashioned, single rose blooms with five petals and in a variety of colours from white to pink. 'Mutabilis' is particularly attractive, slightly larger growing, with large, handsome cup-shaped flowers that are a soft yellow when young, aging to a coppery pink or crimson. Another variety, 'Minima', is very small growing and covered with single or double red, pink, or white flowers in spring and summer. ❀ **PLANTING** Like all roses, *Rosa chinensis* needs plenty of sunshine and moderately rich soil that has had plenty of organic matter added. Mulch well, taking care not to take the mulch layer too close to the plant. ❀ **FLOWERING** Flowers are recurrent from spring through until autumn. ❀ **CULTIVATION** Keep the area around the base of the plant free from weeds and other plants to allow free air circulation, which will help to prevent black spot. Water well in summer if conditions are hot and dry. ❀ **PROPAGATION** From semi-ripe cuttings taken in autumn.

Viburnum tinus
Laurustinus ○ ◑ ❖❖

❀ **DESCRIPTION** A most attractive evergreen shrub with a dense,
bushy habit and a thick covering of oval, deep green foliage. Often grown
as a hedging or screen plant, this viburnum grows to 10 feet (3 m) and has
flat heads of small, white flowers that emerge from pinkish buds that cover
the entire bush. The variety 'Lucidum' has larger and more showy flowers
and a more open growth habit, but will not survive harsh growing
conditions as easily as the species. ❀ **PLANTING** While this viburnum
can be grown in a semi-shaded position, it will produce a more prolific
flower display when in full sun. The soil should be quite deep and fertile,
and capable of holding moisture during hot weather. Good drainage is also
important. ❀ **FLOWERING** Flowers from late winter through to mid-
spring. ❀ **CULTIVATION** After planting, mulch around the base of the
shrub to suppress weed growth and help maintain soil moisture. Water well
in summer if the weather is hot and dry. If growing as a clipped hedge,
prune back after flowering or at the end of summer. ❀ **PROPAGATION**
From semi-ripe cuttings taken in autumn.

Gelsemium sempervirens
False jasmine ○ ◐ ❖❖

✿ **OTHER NAMES** Carolina jasmine, Evening trumpet flower, Jessamine
✿ **DESCRIPTION** A moderately vigorous, evergreen twining climber
that can be used to cover pergolas, archways, or unsightly fences or walls. It
is easy to grow in a wide range of climates and conditions, with a good
covering of lance-shaped, glossy green foliage. It is the flowers, however,
that make this an outstanding vine for the low-maintenance garden. In
summer the plant is covered with showy clusters of funnel-shaped, fragrant
flowers that are in a variety of shades of yellow, from quite pale to a deep,
rich hue. ✿ **PLANTING** Easy to grow in most soils, the Carolina jasmine
likes full sun, however, it will still be quite successful if grown in a semi-
shaded situation. It will not grow where the winters are cold and frosty, but
it is a success in temperate climates. In cold climates it is best grown in a
greenhouse. ✿ **FLOWERING** Flowers over many weeks in summer.
✿ **CULTIVATION** Mulch with an organic mix of well-rotted manures
and compost, which will feed the plant while helping to stop the soil from
drying out in summer. A liquid organic fertilizer, applied in late spring, will
aid flower production. ✿ **PROPAGATION** Can be grown from seed
sown in spring, or from semi-ripe cuttings taken in summer.

Jasminum polyanthum
Chinese jasmine ○ ◑ ❖❖

❧ **OTHER NAME** Pink jasmine ❧ **DESCRIPTION** A delightful woody-stemmed, evergreen twining climber that is wonderfully fragrant and should be grown on trellis or archways near the house, from where its fragrance can be easily enjoyed. It is quite a vigorous and easy-to-grow vine that will quickly cover a fence or garden shed and hide it from view. The stems are well covered with dark green leaves, and for many weeks the entire vine is covered with clusters of small, white, fragrant flowers sometimes tinged with red on the outsides. The flowers are especially fragrant in the sun. ❧ **PLANTING** For best results, plant in moderately rich and well-drained soil that has been enriched with organic matter. Water well until established, and provide support for the plant to twine and climb. In cold climates it is best planted in a greenhouse. ❧ **FLOWERING** Flowers for long periods from late spring well into summer. ❧ **CULTIVATION** Water in summer if conditions are hot and dry, and mulch to help retain soil moisture. Trimming back may be necessary if the plant grows too large where it is climbing, or too invasive. ❧ **PROPAGATION** From semi-ripe cuttings taken in summer.

Pelargonium peltatum
Ivy-leaf geranium ○ ❖

❀ **OTHER NAME** Hanging geranium ❀ **DESCRIPTION** A charming
and robust trailing climber that is only grown as a house plant in areas that
experience cold or frosty winters. A native of the Mediterranean, this trailing
geranium is useful for growing in hanging baskets or window boxes that get
plenty of direct sunshine. It has attractive fleshy leaves with pointed lobes,
similar to ivy, hence the common name. The flowers are single and either
mauve or white in colour. Cultivars include 'Amethyst', which has large,
double flowers that are light purple-mauve in colour; and 'D'Elegante',
which has variegated foliage and pink flowers. Many other cultivars are
available, some that trail 3 feet (1 m) over the side of a bank or hanging
basket. ❀ **PLANTING** Ivy-leaf geraniums must have plenty of warm sun
and well-drained soil or potting mixture that is moderately rich and capable
of holding moisture in summer. Mulch after planting, and water deeply
when the weather is hot and dry. In cold climates plant as a summer annual.
❀ **FLOWERING** Flowers over many months during late spring, summer,
and early autumn. ❀ **CULTIVATION** A very easy plant to keep once well
established. Trim off dead foliage and spent flowers, and mulch to stop the
soil from drying out. ❀ **PROPAGATION** Very easy to propagate from
softwood cuttings taken from spring to autumn.

Schizophragma hydrangeoides

Japanese hydrangea vine ○ ◑ ❖❖❖

✿ **DESCRIPTION** A useful, deciduous, woody-stemmed root climber that is sometimes confused with *Hydrangea anomala petiolaris*, although they are quite separate species. The Japanese hydrangea vine can grow quite vigorously to 18 feet (5.4 m) in height, and is often used to cover unslightly walls or buildings. The foliage is large and broadly oval, with a serrated margin. The flowers are small, white or creamy-white, and are surrounded by sterile flowers that have heart-shaped, light yellow sepals. The effect, when in flower, is quite delightful. ✿ **PLANTING** To produce good results, plant in moderately fertile soil that has had plenty of organic matter in the form of well-rotted animal manures or compost added to it. Good drainage is important, and the planting area may need to be built up above ground level to create good growing conditions. ✿ **FLOWERING** Flowers prolifically in summer. ✿ **CULTIVATION** Water well until plants are established, and keep watering during hot, dry conditions. Mulch with leaf litter, and trim back any stray branches. ✿ **PROPAGATION** Can be grown from seed planted in spring, or from semi-ripe cuttings taken in summer.

Achillea filipendulina

Yarrow ○ ❖❖❖

❀ **OTHER NAMES** Fernleaf yarrow, Milfoil ❀ **DESCRIPTION** An excellent and easy-to-grow upright perennial that is good for sunny flowerbeds and borders or as part of a rockery garden. This species can grow to 4 feet (1.2 m) in height, and spreads rapidly to form a handsome clump. It has a graceful appearance, with fern-like, greyish-green foliage and showy heads of small, golden yellow flowers that hold their colour well when cut and dried. There are several varieties, including 'Parker's Variety', which has bright yellow flowers, and 'Cherry Plate', which has very large flower heads in the cherry-red range. ❀ **PLANTING** A very adaptable plant in most soils and climates, yarrow will thrive in a sunny, open position is moderately fertile and well-drained soil. Allow space around the plant for it to spread. ❀ **FLOWERING** Flowers appear over many weeks in summer. ❀ **CULTIVATION** A very low-maintenance plant, yarrow will survive even when neglected. Taller varieties may need staking if planted in an exposed, windy area. ❀ **PROPAGATION** As the plant spreads, the clump can be easily divided and planted around the garden. This can be done in autumn or late winter–early spring.

Aquilegia vulgaris
Columbine ○ ◑ ❖❖❖

✿ **OTHER NAME** European columbine, Granny's bonnet

✿ **DESCRIPTION** A worthwhile, short-lived, clump-forming herbaceous perennial that is charming in a mixed flowerbed or border, or as part of a woodland garden. *Aquilegia vulgaris* is very popular in Europe, where it can be found growing wild. Reaching 18 inches (4 cm) in height, it forms a clump of deeply divided, greyish-green foliage with fascinating short-spurred, bell-shaped flowers that can be blue, purple, or white in colour. The plant dies down and disappears underground in winter, reappearing the following spring. ✿ **PLANTING** In most gardens, columbines like an open, sunny position, however, if summer conditions are hot, some provision for shade should be made. Any good garden soil is suitable, preferably with good drainage and an ability to hold moisture in summer.

✿ **FLOWERING** Flowers appear in late spring and early summer.

✿ **CULTIVATION** Columbine does not last indefinitely, and will need to be replaced every few years. After the foliage dies back, add a layer of well-rotted manure to the ground. Water well in summer if conditions are dry.

✿ **PROPAGATION** By seed in autumn or spring.

Armeria maritima
Thrift ○ ❖❖❖

✿ **OTHER NAMES** Sea pink, Armeria, Cliff rose

✿ **DESCRIPTION** A hardy and useful clump-forming evergreen perennial that can be used as an edging in rockery gardens or as part of a mixed flowerbed or border. Thrift forms an attractive clump of narrow, grass-like, mid-green foliage, from which emerge stiff stems that carry delightful, circular flower heads in various shades of pink and white. It grows to 6 inches (15 cm) in height, and can be mass-planted to great effect. The variety 'Laucheana' has outstanding, deep crimson flower heads.

✿ **PLANTING** Easy to grow in a wide range of soil conditions, providing good drainage is present. Choose a sunny, open position and build up beds with organic matter if drainage is poor. ✿ **FLOWERING** Flowers for many weeks during late spring and summer. ✿ **CULTIVATION** Mulch around plants to keep weed growth to a minimum and to prevent the soil surface from drying out in summer. Remove spent flower stems to encourage further flowering. ✿ **PROPAGATION** From semi-ripe cuttings in summer, or from seed gathered in autumn.

Bergenia cordifolia
Heartleaf bergenia ○ ◑ ❖❖❖

✿ **DESCRIPTION** A native of Siberia, this clump-forming, evergreen perennial is valued both for its attractive foliage and flowers. Bergenia can be mass-planted as a ground cover, or, because it likes moist soil conditions, can be used for edging pools or streams. Heartleaf bergenia has rounded, puckered foliage with crinkled edges and a leathery texture, and racemes of small, mauve-pink, cup-shaped flowers. The flowers are held above the foliage on slender but sturdy stems. Varieties include 'Purpurea', which has purple-tinged foliage and magenta flowers, and 'Red', which has deep carmine flowers.
✿ **PLANTING** Choose a sheltered, semi-shaded position in preference to full sun, which seems to retard growth. The soil can be quite poor, which seems to produce stronger leaf colour, although it should be able to hold moisture and provide good drainage. ✿ **FLOWERING** Flowers bloom in late winter and spring. ✿ **CULTIVATION** This hardy plant requires very little attention once established, except for extra watering during hot, dry summers. ✿ **PROPAGATION** Easily propagated by division, which should be done after flowering has finished in spring.

Helleborus orientalis
Lenten rose ◐ ● ❖❖❖

✿ **OTHER NAME** Winter rose ✿ **DESCRIPTION** The lenten rose is one of the most highly prized woodland perennials, because it begins to flower in late winter and continues flowering through most of spring. A native of Asia Minor, it is an evergreen, clump-forming perennial that grows to 18 inches (45 cm), with large, palmate leaves held erect on stems, and nodding, cup-shaped flowers in various shades of greenish white through to pink and deep purple. Some flowers are marked with deep purple spots. Lenten roses are most effect when mass-planted beneath trees in a woodland garden or as feature plants in shady areas where little else will grow. ✿ **PLANTING** Choose a sheltered, shady position and ensure that the soil has been enriched with plenty of well-rotted organic matter prior to planting. Conditions must be rich, moist, and well-drained for success. ✿ **FLOWERING** Flowers in late winter and spring.
✿ **CULTIVATION** Water well in summer, as the hellebore resents the soil drying out in hot weather. Trim off last year's foliage just as the plant begins to flower. New leaves will form after the flowering. Protect from snails and slugs. ✿ **PROPAGATION** From seed, or by dividing plants in spring or early autumn.

Hosta plantaginea
Plaintain lily ● ❖❖❖

✿ **OTHER NAMES** Funkia, August lily ✿ **DESCRIPTION** Hostas
are highly prized foliage plants that can be used in various ways—for example,
to edge pathways and borders, or to surround pools, ponds, or streams. This
particular species is native to Japan, and is the only hosta with fragrant
flowers, making it ideal for planting in a shaded area beside a gazebo or
outdoor entertaining area where its fragrance can be easily enjoyed. It forms
a dense clump of foliage that emerges directly from the ground, then dies
back in winter. The leaves are large, bright green and glossy, while the small,
pure-white, scented flowers are held above the foliage on slender stems.
✿ **PLANTING** Hostas must have moderately rich, moist, well-drained
soil that has been dug deeply and enriched with plenty of organic matter.
Choose a shady position, and mulch well at planting time to retain soil
moisture. ✿ **FLOWERING** Flowers during late summer and autumn.
✿ **CULTIVATION** Snails and slugs adore hosta foliage, so protection
from these pests is essential. Mulch around plants as they grow, and water
well if the summer conditions are dry. After the foliage dies back, feed
with a layer of well-rotted manure to boost new growth in spring.
✿ **PROPAGATION** By division of clumps in early spring.

Lavandula angustifolia (syn. *Lavandula officinalis*)
English lavender ○ ❖❖❖

❀ **OTHER NAME** True lavender ❀ **DESCRIPTION** One of the most popular of all fragrant evergreen perennial herbs, true lavender can be used as a low-growing hedge or border, as part of a traditional herb garden, or as a companion plant to roses. Growing to 3 feet (1 m) in height, it has an open, irregular outline and upright stems covered with small, greyish, furry leaves that age to mid-green in colour. The small flowers are held on slender, upright spikes, and are lavender-mauve and highly fragrant. Varieties include 'Alba', which has white flowers; 'Hidcote', which has deep purple flowers and silvery-grey foliage; and 'Munstead Dwarf', which has blue-purple flowers. ❀ **PLANTING** Plenty of sunshine and moderately rich, well-drained soil will provide the appropriate growing conditions for lavender. If drainage is poor, create built-up beds with plenty of well-rotted compost, and water deeply in summer to encourage the downward growth of roots. ❀ **FLOWERING** The flowers continue to bloom for several months, from spring through to autumn. ❀ **CULTIVATION** Mulch well to help retain soil moisture, and keep weeds from around the base of the plant. If growing as a hedge or border, trim plants lightly in early spring to encourage dense growth. ❀ **PROPAGATION** From semi-ripe cuttings taken in summer.

Ligularia dentata
Bigleaf golden ray ○ ❖❖❖

✿ **DESCRIPTION** A handsome, clump-forming perennial that grows to 4 feet (1.2 m) and is valued both for its foliage and charming, daisy-like flowers. It can be used in a mixed bed or flower border, or as an accent plant at the edge of the garden. A native of China and Japan, this species has very large, brownish-green, kidney-shaped leaves that are a deep red-brown on the undersides. During summer it bears clusters of large, showy, yellow-orange flowers on branching stems held high above the foliage.

✿ **PLANTING** This rugged plant does well in most soils, providing drainage is adequate. Choose a sunny, open position and add plenty of organic matter at planting time to improve the soil fertility. ✿ **FLOWERING** Flowers begin to bloom in summer. ✿ **CULTIVATION** Mulch around the plant when established to help prevent the soil from drying out in summer. Keep a watch on snails and slugs, which enjoy feasting on the foliage.

✿ **PROPAGATION** By division of clumps in spring, or from seed sown in autumn or spring.

Limonium sinuatum
Sea lavender ○ ❖❖❖

✿ **OTHER NAMES** Notch-leaf statice ✿ **DESCRIPTION** This
attractive, bushy perennial is usually cultivated as an annual or biennial,
depending on the climate where it is grown. Reaching 2 feet (60 cm) in
height, it has lance-shaped, mid-green leaves and clusters of small, tubular
flowers that can be a variety of hues, including pink, yellow, white, and blue.
Sea lavender is a good plant for cutting and drying for indoor arrangements,
and the flowers will retain their colour for many months. It looks most
effective when planted en masse, or as part of a mixed flowerbed or sunny
border. The flower colours are very bright, so take care they do not clash
with other plants. ✿ **PLANTING** Sea lavender needs plenty of warm
sunshine and well-drained soils. As a native of the Mediterranean region, it
must have warmth and light, friable soil. ✿ **FLOWERING** Flowers from
summer through to early autumn. ✿ **CULTIVATION** Once established,
statice will require very little attention. A mulch layer will keep weed growth
down, and watering in summer is only required if the plant becomes
stressed. ✿ **PROPAGATION** Easy to propagate by division in spring or
from seed sown in autumn or early spring.

Physalis alkekengi
Chinese lantern ○ ◑ ❖❖❖

✿ **OTHER NAMES** Winter cherry, Strawberry ground cherry

✿ **DESCRIPTION** The *Physalis* genus includes an interesting group of perennials, and sometimes annuals, that are grown for their unusual calyces and fruits rather than for their foliage or flowers. This species is a hardy, spreading perennial that can be grown as an annual. It reaches 2 feet (60 cm) in height, with mid-green foliage that is oval in shape. In summer the plant produces inconspicuous, white, star-shaped flowers, which are followed by a display of bright, orange-red fruits surrounded by vivid orange calyces. Statice can look most effective as a feature plant in a mixed flower border.

✿ **PLANTING** This adaptable plant will grow well either in a sunny, open position or in partial shade, providing the soil is moderately rich and well-drained. Prepare the soil well prior to planting, by digging in plenty of well-rotted compost. ✿ **FLOWERING** Flowers appear in summer, followed by fruits in autumn. ✿ **CULTIVATION** Water well if the summer is hot and dry. Mulch around plants to keep weed growth down.

✿ **PROPAGATION** Either by division or from softwood cuttings taken in spring.

Thymus vulgaris
Garden thyme ○ ❖❖❖

❀ **DESCRIPTION** One of the most popular and easy-to-grow aromatic perennial herbs, which can be cultivated in many ways. Thyme is an excellent potted plant, cascading over the edge of the container, or it can be planted between pavers to create a wonderful wafting fragrance when walked upon. It is also an important inclusion in the herb garden. Thyme is a low-growing, ground-covering herb with slender stems and masses of tiny, evergreen greyish leaves that are highly aromatic. For many weeks in summer it is covered with small, lilac-purple flowers that are borne on small, upright spikes. Thyme is also a useful plant for binding together steep banks, or for growing in a rockery garden. ❀ **PLANTING** The best position is in full sun, and the soil needs to be reasonably fertile, with good drainage. In gardens with heavy soil, plenty of well-rotted compost and manure should be added to lift and aerate the soil. Soils that are very sandy should also have organic matter added, to help them retain moisture after watering or rainfall. ❀ **FLOWERING** Flowers bloom over many months from early summer. ❀ **CULTIVATION** Mulch around plants to keep the soil surface free from weeds, and to help prevent the ground from drying out in summer. Water during dry weather, and prune lightly in spring if stems become lax or straggly. ❀ **PROPAGATION** From semi-ripe or softwood cuttings taken in summer.

Arum italicum

Lords and ladies ○ ◑ ❖❖

✿ **OTHER NAME** Italian arum ✿ **DESCRIPTION** Lords and ladies are an easy-to-grow and useful group of bulbs with attractive foliage and flowers. They can be grown in large clumps as features in mixed beds or flower borders, or used as accent plants in shady areas of the garden. The Italian arum is noted for its handsome, upright, arrow-shaped foliage, reaching a height of 1 foot (30 cm). The flowers are less dramatic, being small and white and borne on thick, fleshy stems. They are followed by striking red fruits in autumn, which cover a large area of the stem. The variety 'Pictum' has bright green leaves with cream or white-marked veins, followed by creamy-white spathes and then red berries. ✿ **PLANTING** This bulb needs rich, moist soil that has good drainage. Choose a sunny or semi-shaded position, and add plenty of well-rotted compost or manure to the soil before planting. ✿ **FLOWERING** Flowers appear in summer, followed by berries in autumn. ✿ **CULTIVATION** When mature they will require very little attention, apart from watering in midsummer if conditions are hot and dry. ✿ **PROPAGATION** By sowing seed collected in autumn, or from division of clumps in early spring.

Colchicum autumnale
Autumn crocus ○ ◐ ❖❖❖

✿ **OTHER NAME** Meadow saffron ✿ **DESCRIPTION** One of the
most delightful of all the corms, the colchicum group are commonly called
'crocus' and are grown in many ways to bring a sudden touch of colour to
the autumn garden. They can be mass-planted in lawns or beneath trees
where some sunshine is present, or used at the front of a garden bed or
rockery. They are also excellent plants for shallow terracotta pots. Growing
to a height of 6 inches (15 cm), the flowers of *Colchicum autumnale* are
quite large and showy, goblet-shaped, and rosy-purple. The leaves are strap-
like and mid-green, and appear after the flowers have finished. There is a
white flowering variety called 'alba', and also a double white flowering
variety that is more difficult to obtain. ✿ **PLANTING** Good drainage is
essential for colchicums, as for most bulbs and corms. Plant the corms in full
sun or dappled shade, in rich, moist, well-drained soil. Cover the soil surface
with leaf mulch. ✿ **FLOWERING** Flowers, without foliage, pop up
through the soil in autumn. ✿ **CULTIVATION** Avoid overwatering the
area where the corms are planted, especially if the ground is not well-
drained. Lift and divide offsets every few years. ✿ **PROPAGATION** By
seed, or by division of offsets in autumn.

Convallaria majalis
Lily-of-the-valley ◑ ❖❖❖

❀ **DESCRIPTION** A wonderful plant for a shady, woodland garden, the lily-of-the-valley is highly fragrant and delightful when naturalized beneath deciduous trees or along woodland paths. It is a very popular species, native to Europe, Asia, and North America. Lily-of-the-valley can grow to a height of 8 inches (20 cm), with the large, oval, mid-green leaves emerging from the base of the plant, seemingly directly out of the ground. Slender spikes rise from within the curve of the foliage, carrying delightfully fragrant, white, waxy, bell-like flowers. A variety called 'Rosea' has similar foliage, but the flowers are a very pale purplish-pink. ❀ **PLANTING** Lily-of-the-valley rhizomes are sown in autumn, into any reasonable garden soil that is well-drained. However, they will do better if the soil is rich in humus and moisture retentive. A semi-shaded situation is preferable. ❀ **FLOWERING** Flowers from late spring to early summer, depending on the climate.

❀ **CULTIVATION** Once naturalized, these plants require very little maintenance. In autumn, an application of well-rotted manure over the soil surface will produce good results the following spring. ❀ **PROPAGATION** Easy to propagate by division after flowering, or by planting of corms in autumn.

Crocosmia x *crocosmiiflora*

Montbretia ○ ❖❖

❀ **DESCRIPTION** A native of South Africa, this handsome group of corms belongs to the Iris family, and is closely linked to the charming tritonias. Grown mainly for their showy flowers, this species reaches 3 feet (1 m) in height, forming a dense clump of mid-green, sword-like leaves. The flowers are carried on arching spikes, and each bloom is tubular and in the orange or yellow colour range. Many beautiful hybrids have been raised, including 'Aurora', which has vivid orange flowers; 'Her Majesty', which has very large crimson-scarlet flowers with yellow centres; and 'Lord Nelson', which has orange-scarlet blooms. ❀ **PLANTING** These are very durable bulbs that can be rather invasive, as they multiply freely in areas where they feel at home. Any reasonable, well-drained, friable garden loam is suitable, and preferably, the position should be open and sunny. ❀ **FLOWERING** Flowers appear for many weeks in summer. ❀ **CULTIVATION** Once established, little maintenance is required apart from dividing clumps that have become dense and overgrown. In very cold climates they may be lifted and stored over winter. ❀ **PROPAGATION** Easy to divide in early spring, just as the foliage growth begins.

Cyclamen hederifolium

Neapolitan cyclamen ◐ ❖❖❖

✿ **DESCRIPTION** Cyclamens are charming plants that may be difficult to establish, however, once they have nestled into a comfortable position they will require very little care and attention. Growing to 4 inches (10 cm) in height, the Neapolitan cyclamen forms an attractive clump of ivy-shaped, bright green foliage, often with silvery-green markings. The pale to deep pink flowers are absolutely delightful, held above the foliage on slender stems. The Neapolitan cyclamen can be planted in a shady rockery or woodland garden, or naturalized en masse beneath deciduous trees. The flowers and foliage die back in winter. ✿ **PLANTING** Plant seed in late summer or autumn into well-prepared soil that has good drainage and plenty of well-rotted organic matter added. The soil must be capable of holding moisture without ever becoming waterlogged. ✿ **FLOWERING** Late summer and autumn are the flowering periods. ✿ **CULTIVATION** Take care not to overwater in summer. After the foliage and flowers have died back, mulch the soil surface with well-rotted leaf mulch. ✿ **PROPAGATION** Propagated by seed sown in late summer or autumn.

Erythronium americanum

Trout lily ◐ ❖❖❖

✿ **OTHER NAMES** Common fawn lily, Amberbell

✿ **DESCRIPTION** A worthwhile group of tuberous perennials, grown for their attractive foliage and pendant flowers. Native to North America, they are sometimes called dogtooth violets, but resemble small lilies more closely. Growing to 1 foot (30 cm) in height, the fleshy, semi-erect foliage is mottled green and brown, while the large yellow flowers are held above the foliage on slender stems. The flowers are yellow and bronze, with petals that curl back in sunlight, giving them a starry appearance. These plants are most attractive when planted in clumps or naturalized in the shade of deciduous trees. ✿ **PLANTING** Autumn is the best planting time. Prepare the soil with plenty of organic matter, as these plants require humus-rich, well-drained soil that does not dry out in summer. When replanting tubers, do not allow them to dry out. ✿ **FLOWERING** The flowers appear in mid-spring. ✿ **CULTIVATION** Mulch around the plants well to prevent the soil from becoming too hot or too dry during summer. Some shade in warm climates may be necessary. Water well when dry. ✿ **PROPAGATION** From seed or tubers planted in autumn.

Fritillaria meleagris
Snake's head fritillary   ○ ◐ ❖❖❖

❀ **OTHER NAMES** Guinea-hen flower, Leper lily

❀ **DESCRIPTION** This is a fascinating bulb, admired for its unusual, bell-shaped drooping flowers. It makes a good talking point in a woodland or cottage garden, planted in a small group or drift for a pleasing effect. Native to California, the snake's head fritillary grows to a height of 1 foot (30 cm) with scattered, slender, greyish-green foliage and large, purplish, drooping flowers that are sometimes mottled. There is also a white form, 'Aphrodite', which has larger and more showy blooms, and is better grown in partial shade where the petals will not be scorched by the sun.

❀ **PLANTING** This bulb is easy to grow, either in the sun or dappled shade, providing the soil is light and well-drained so that it will not be damp in summer when the bulb is dormant. Place the bulb in the planting hole at an angle, so that moisture is not trapped in the hole on the top, which can cause bulb rot. ❀ **FLOWERING** Flowers in spring.

❀ **CULTIVATION** This is an easycare plant if the right conditions are provided. Take care not to overwater in summer. ❀ **PROPAGATION** Either by offsets in summer, or from seed in autumn or winter.

Hyacinthoides hispanica (syn. *Scilla campanulata*)
Spanish bluebell ◑ ❖❖❖

✿ **OTHER NAMES** Spanish hyacinth, Wood hyacinth, Spanish squill
✿ **DESCRIPTION** A very durable group of bulbs that are grown for
their delightful bluebell flowers. Spanish bluebells can be used in many ways
to great effect. They are often seen mass-planted beneath deciduous trees to
create a colourful woodland scene, or in large clumps in a shady bed or border.
The foliage grows to 20 inches (50 cm) in height, as strap-like leaves emerging
from a central clump. From this rises a sturdy stem on which many delightful,
bell-shaped flowers are carried. The flowers are mainly blue, however, pink
and white flower forms are also available. ✿ **PLANTING** Once established,
the Spanish bluebell may become invasive, so care must be taken to select a
site where it cannot take over. Best grown in partial shade in heavy, humus-
rich soil. ✿ **FLOWERING** Expect a dramatic flower display in mid-spring.
✿ **CULTIVATION** This bulb likes plenty of moisture, and care must be
taken to water well, especially if the soil is light or the summer conditions
are hot and dry. After the foliage dies back, feed with a general purpose
fertilizer and allow the foliage to completely yellow and wither—never cut it
away, as the bulb will not flower the following season.
✿ **PROPAGATION** Easy to propagate by division in late summer, or by
sowing seed in autumn.

Narcissus pseudonarcissus

Wild daffodil

✿ **OTHER NAMES** Daffodil, Lent lily, Trumpet narcissus

✿ **DESCRIPTION** Daffodils are prized for their ease of cultivation, making them one of the most popular spring-flowering bulbs in the world. They can be planted in clumps as part of the mixed flowerbed or scattered in drifts beneath deciduous trees to create a woodland garden effect. This particular daffodil, known by several common names, grows to 15 inches (38 cm), with slender, strap-like, mid-green leaves and nodding flowers with clear yellow petals and slightly darker yellow trumpets. ✿ **PLANTING** Good drainage is essential, and therefore, lighter, more friable soils give the best results. If the ground is heavy, incorporate plenty of organic matter and build up beds to improve drainage. Bulbs are planted in autumn, to a depth that is three times the width of the bulb. ✿ **FLOWERING** Flowers bloom from early spring. ✿ **CULTIVATION** Daffodils are very low maintenance and will basically take care of themselves once established. Allow the foliage to wither and die completely after flowering, and sprinkle on some general purpose fertilizer during this process, as it will aid flowering the following season. Every five years or so the clumps may be lifted and divided in autumn if they have become overcrowded or if flowering has diminished.

✿ **PROPAGATION** By division of bulbs in autumn.

Nymphaea alba
White water lily ○ ❖❖❖

❀ **DESCRIPTION** This vigorous, deciduous water lily is a native of Europe and North Africa. It is a hardy water plant that can be grown in a wide range of climates, producing delightful fragrant flowers over many months. The floating foliage is large, circular, and dark green, sometimes a reddish bronze when young. The flowers are quite captivating—large, cup-shaped, semi-double, and pure white. They exude a wonderful fragrance when in sunlight.
❀ **PLANTING** Water lilies can either be planted in containers or in soil at the base of a garden pond. They require a rich soil mix that includes plenty of well-rotted cow manure. If planting in containers, cover the soil surface with gravel to prevent it from floating away in the water. They like a sunny, open position and water that is relatively clear and clean. ❀ **FLOWERING** For long periods in late spring, summer, and early autumn. Flowers bloom for longer periods in warm climates. ❀ **CULTIVATION** Once established, water lilies require very little care and attention, apart from an annual feeding with a slow-release organic fertilizer. ❀ **PROPAGATION** Either from seed, or division of small plantlets in spring or early summer.

Ornithogalum umbellatum
Star of Bethlehem ○ ◑ ❖❖❖

✿ **DESCRIPTION** An interesting group of easy-to-grow bulbs that is valued for the starry white flowers. They can be used as feature plants in a sunny flowerbed or border garden, or planted in dappled sunlight as a woodland bulb, where they will rapidly multiply and spread. Growing to 1 foot (30 cm), this plant forms an attractive mound of foliage, each leaf being smooth, slender, and mid-green. The flower stalks rise from the centre of this mound, and are crowned with up to 20 white, star-like flowers, their outer segments striped with green. ✿ **PLANTING** Like many bulbs, star-of-Bethlehem will do well in soil that is well-drained and has been enriched with some well-rotted manure or compost. Choose a sunny or semi-shaded position, and plant offsets during autumn in well-prepared ground. ✿ **FLOWERING** Flowers appear in mid-spring.
✿ **CULTIVATION** Mulch with leaf litter, and take care not to overwater in summer. Allow the foliage to completely wither and die back after flowering, and sprinkle with a general purpose fertilizer to encourage good flowering the following season. ✿ **PROPAGATION** Easy to propagate from offsets in autumn.

Scilla peruviana
Cuban lily ○ ◑ ❖❖❖

DESCRIPTION A handsome bulb that is hardy and easy to grow in a wide variety of climates and situations. Growing to a height of 10 inches (25 cm), the Cuban lily emerges as a basal cluster of lance-shaped, semi-erect foliage, from which the flower stems rise. The stems are topped by conical flower heads, each carrying many small, violet-blue flowers that create a wonderful display. It can be naturalized in a semi-shaded area of the garden, or grown as a feature plant in beds with other bulbs or flowering perennials. ❧ **PLANTING** Like most spring-flowering bulbs, the Cuban lily should be planted in autumn into ground that has been dug over and enriched with plenty of organic matter. Good drainage is essential, and the bulbs should be watered in after planting, taking care not to overwater.
❧ **FLOWERING** The flowers appear in spring. ❧ **CULTIVATION** Very little care or maintenance will be necessary once the bulbs have become established. If overcrowding occurs, lift and divide the plants in late summer or autumn. ❧ **PROPAGATION** Either by division of clumps at the end of summer, or from planting the bulbs in autumn.

Zantedeschia aethiopica

Arum lily ○ ◑ ❖

✿ **OTHER NAMES** White arum lily, Lily of the Nile, Common calla
✿ **DESCRIPTION** One of the most popular of all garden bulbs, the
arum, or calla, lily is easy to grow in temperate and warm climates, where it
should remain in leaf all year round. In cooler districts the foliage disappears
in winter. Native to South Africa, the common calla grows to 3 feet (1 m) in
height, forming a large clump of broad, arrow-shaped, bright green leaves.
The flowers are actually spathes, and they emerge on fleshy stems through
the foliage. They are white, with a yellow spadix. varieties include 'Green
Goddess', which has dramatic green and white spathes, and 'Crowborough',
which has slightly darker foliage. ✿ **PLANTING** This charming plant
must have plenty of moisture to perform at its best, and can even be planted
successfully in boggy soil at the margins of garden pools or streams. Add
plenty of organic matter to the soil, and water well in summer if conditions
are hot and dry. ✿ **FLOWERING** Flowers appear prolifically in late spring
and early summer. ✿ **CULTIVATION** Once established little care is
required, apart from summer watering and lifting and dividing clumps that
become too overcrowded. ✿ **PROPAGATION** Easy to propagate from
offsets taken in late autumn or winter.

Aubrieta deltoidea

Aubrieta ○ ❖❖❖

❀ **OTHER NAME** Purple rock cress ❀ **DESCRIPTION** A member of the mustard family, this ground-covering plant forms a dense mat of foliage that looks most attractive at the edge of a flowerbed or border, or as part of a sunny, rockery garden. The evergreen foliage is bright green, sometimes variegated, and the small flowers are borne recurrently throughout the main growing season. The flowers are in the red to purple colour range. The variety 'Argenteo-variegata' has cream and green variegated foliage and pink-lavender flowers. ❀ **PLANTING** This reliable small plant will thrive in any soil that is well-drained, even withstanding dry backs and rockery gardens that do not get much summer watering. Plant in spring or summer, and water lightly until plants become firmly established.

❀ **FLOWERING** Flowers in spring and early summer, followed by a flowering in autumn. ❀ **CULTIVATION** Once established this ground cover is easy to maintain. Keep weeds from around the base of the plant by mulching, which will also encourage it to spread. Trim back hard after the spring flowering to encourage a second flush of flowers in autumn.

❀ **PROPAGATION** Can be propagated from greenwood cuttings taken in summer, from semi-ripe cuttings taken in autumn, or from seed sown from spring to autumn, depending on the climate.

Campanula poscharskyana
Bellflower   ○ ◐ ● ❖❖❖

✿ **OTHER NAME** Serbian bellflower ✿ **DESCRIPTION** A vigorous, evergreen trailing perennial that looks beautiful at the front of a flowerbed, border, or as part of a rockery garden in dappled shade. Growing to 4 inches (10 cm) in height, it makes a good ground cover of small, ivy-shaped mid-green leaves, topped by showy clusters of large, bell-shaped flowers in a rich shade of violet. ✿ **PLANTING** Campanulas must have moderately rich, moist, and well-drained soil mixed with plenty of rotted manure or compost to help retain moisture. A semi-shaded position is preferable, to bring out the brilliance of the violet flowers, however, planting in full sun will also produce good results. ✿ **FLOWERING** Flowers bloom in late spring and early summer. ✿ **CULTIVATION** Mulch around the young plants to help keep weed growth down and to prevent the soil from drying out in summer. Water if conditions are hot and dry, and protect foliage growth from snails and slugs, which can be quite a problem. ✿ **PROPAGATION** By softwood cuttings taken in spring, or by division in either autumn or spring. Can also be grown from seed sown in spring.

Convolvulus cneorum

Ground morning glory ○ ❖

✿ **OTHER NAME** Silver bush ✿ **DESCRIPTION** A delightful,
although tender, rounded, bushy and evergreen shrub that can only be grown
in warm to hot climates. Ideal as a rockery plant, or garden edging, it grows
to 4 feet (1.2 m) with narrow, silky, silvery-green leaves and wonderfully
showy white flowers with yellow centres. The flowers begin as pink-tinged
buds, then open out to pure-white blooms. ✿ **PLANTING** This plant will
do extremely well, even in quite poor soils, providing the drainage is adequate.
Choose a sunny, open, and well-drained position, and plant in spring when
all danger of frost has passed. Water until established, then reduce watering
to encourage deep root growth. ✿ **FLOWERING** Flowers from mid-spring
to late summer. ✿ **CULTIVATION** Mulch around plants, taking care not
to take the mulch layer too close to the main stem. The flowering season can
be extended by regular deadheading of spent blooms.
✿ **PROPAGATION** Can be grown from seed planted in mid-spring, or
from softwood cuttings taken in spring or summer.

Dianthus deltoides
Maiden pink ○ p̂H ❖❖❖

❀ **DESCRIPTION** An evergreen, mat-forming, tufted perennial that can be mass-planted to great effect at the front of a sunny flowerbed, or used as a feature plant in a rockery garden. It can, in time, become invasive, and care must be taken that it does not overwhelm other plants. Growing to a height of 6 inches (15 cm), it forms a vigorous mat of grassy foliage, from which slender flower spikes emerge, topped by small white, pink, or cerise single flowers. ❀ **PLANTING** Pinks will thrive in an open, sunny position in light, friable soil that has good drainage. In gardens with heavy soil, build up beds or add plenty of well-rotted organic matter to improve the soil texture. Water well until the plants are established.

❀ **FLOWERING** Flowers from spring to early summer.

❀ **CULTIVATION** Water during hot, dry summer weather, and mulch to reduce the evaporation of moisture from the soil. Trim back flowers to encourage further flowering. Keep a close watch for aphids which can spread viral diseases, and also watch out for rust and red spider mites. Some of the cultivars are more disease resistant than the species. ❀ **PROPAGATION** By layering stems or from cuttings taken in summer.

Gaultheria procumbens

Checkerberry ◔ ● pH̬ ❖❖❖

❀ **OTHER NAME** Wintergreen, Partridge berry

❀ **DESCRIPTION** A native, evergreen subshrub found growing in the woods in eastern North America, this delightful, low-growing species is used as a natural ground cover in shaded garden beds or woodland gardens. Growing to 3 inches (7 cm) in height, it spreads rapidly, covering the soil surface with clusters of oval, leathery leaves that become red in winter. The small white flowers, flushed with pink, are followed by attractive scarlet red berries. ❀ **PLANTING** This plant requires a rich, moist, and peaty soil that has a slightly acid pH level. Add well-rotted leaf mulch to the ground prior to planting, to ensure adequate drainage. Choose a shady or semi-shaded position protected from midsummer sun. ❀ **FLOWERING** Flowers appear in summer, followed by berries in autumn. ❀ **CULTIVATION** The soil should never be allowed to completely dry out, especially during summer. Mulch with pine needles or other well-rotted leaf material, which will help keep the ground damp. ❀ **PROPAGATION** Either propagated by semi-ripe cuttings taken in summer, or from seed sown in autumn.

Iberis sempervirens
Perennial candytuft ○ ❖❖❖

❁ **OTHER NAME** Evergreen candytuft ❁ **DESCRIPTION** A charming, old-fashioned subshrub that looks marvellous at the front of a mixed perennial border, or mass-planted to give a carpet of white in late spring. Growing to 1 foot (30 cm) in height, the slender stems spread out, covered with narrow, dark green foliage. The dense, rounded flower heads are pure-white, and look particularly pretty in the early evening. Candytuft can also be grown in a container, placed in a sunny position. ❁ **PLANTING** An easy-to-grow plant that thrives in any moderately rich and well-drained soil. Sow seeds in autumn, or transplant young plants in early spring, allowing space for them to grow and spread. Water well until established. ❁ **FLOWERING** Flowers from mid-spring through to early summer. ❁ **CULTIVATION** A very easy-care plant once established, that will spread and form a pleasant clump unaided. Weeds can sometimes thrive between the stems, and these can be suppressed with a good layer of mulch. Water well in summer to encourage roots to travel downwards. Trim back foliage after flowering has finished. ❁ **PROPAGATION** From seed sown in autumn, or from semi-ripe cuttings taken in summer.

Juniperus horizontalis

Creeping juniper ○ pH ❖❖❖

❀ **DESCRIPTION** A very useful, prostrate, spreading conifer that forms a shrubby mat of foliage up to 18 inches (45 cm) thick. Ideal for sloping banks, rockery gardens, and as the edging of sunny borders, this plant is easy to grow in even quite poor conditions. Creeping juniper is a hardy plant with needle-like, aromatic, blue-green or grey-green foliage, and it also has small blue berries in spring. Cultivars include 'Glauca', which has blue-green foliage all year round; 'Blue Rug', which has outstanding blue foliage; and 'Douglasii', which has blue foliage that turns purple in winter.
❀ **PLANTING** This hardy plant will grow well in a wide variety of soils and conditions, however, it must have good drainage and the soil should be either neutral or slightly alkaline. Choose a sunny, open position and mulch well after planting. ❀ **FLOWERING** Berries appear in spring on new foliage growth. ❀ **CULTIVATION** Once established this plant requires little maintenance, although keep a close watch for rust disease, which can be a problem. ❀ **PROPAGATION** From hardwood cuttings taken in autumn.

Lithodora diffusa (syn. *Lithospermum diffusum*)
'Heavenly Blue' ○ ◑ pH ❖❖❖

✿ **DESCRIPTION** A charming, prostrate shrub with trailing stems that cascade over rocks or garden edges, making it a delightful plant for use as an edging or in a rockery garden. Growing to 6 inches (15 cm) in height, it forms a thick mat of small, hairy, mid-green leaves. The flowers are profuse, covering the entire plant for many weeks in the main growing season. This variety, 'Heavenly Blue', has showy, funnel-shaped flowers in a rich shade of deep blue. Flowers appear more vivid in shady areas, however, the plant can still grow well in full sun. ✿ **PLANTING** The soil should be rich, moist, and well-drained to produce good results. Choose a sheltered, semi-shaded position and add plenty of well-rotted leaf litter to the ground prior to planting. Mulch and water well until established. ✿ **FLOWERING** Flowers appear for long periods in late spring and summer. ✿ **CULTIVATION** Keep well mulched, and do not allow the soil to dry out in summer. This plant will not transplant easily, and resents root disturbance. ✿ **PROPAGATION** From semi-ripe cuttings taken in midsummer, or from seeds sown in autumn.

Phlox subulata
Moss phlox ○ ◑ ❖❖❖

✿ **OTHER NAMES** Moss pink, Ground pink, Mountain phlox
✿ **DESCRIPTION** A low-growing, evergreen perennial that is easy to cultivate and useful in rockery gardens or as a border in mixed flowerbeds. Reaching 6 inches (15 cm) in height, it forms a mound or dense mat of foliage that makes it difficult for weeds to get through, which is why it is valued in rockery gardens. Short, flowering branches emerge above the foliage, which are covered with a profusion of blooms over many weeks. These flowers are star-like, and are white, pink, or mauve. The variety 'Marjory' is particularly attractive, with masses of rose-pink flowers.
✿ **PLANTING** Choose a sunny, open position and ensure that the soil is moderately rich with good drainage. Prepare the area well prior to planting by adding well-rotted organic matter, and water well until the plants are established. If the soil is very light and sandy, position the plants in semi-shade so that the ground will not dry out too quickly. ✿ **FLOWERING** Flowers appear in profusion from early to late spring. ✿ **CULTIVATION** Water well during hot, dry conditions and trim back lightly after flowering.
✿ **PROPAGATION** Plants can be divided after flowering, or propagated by cuttings taken in autumn.

Saxifraga x *urbium* (syn. *Saxifraga umbrosa*)
London pride ◐ ❖❖

❀ **DESCRIPTION** A popular and useful ground-covering or rockery plant that is easy to cultivate if provided with the correct growing conditions. London pride grows to 1 foot (30 cm) in height, forming a rosette of spreading, evergreen foliage. The leaves are spoon-shaped, leathery, and mid-green in colour. The slender flower stems are topped by tiny, star-shaped, white flowers with red spots, which are sometimes flushed with pink. The variety 'Primuloides' is small, however, its deep pink flowers are larger and more showy. ❀ **PLANTING** Saxifraga must have good drainage and can be grown in quite gravelly soils provided some moderately rich humus has been incorporated. The soil must be capable of holding moisture, and some protection is required from strong midday sun, which is why a semi-shaded position is preferable. ❀ **FLOWERING** Flowers bloom during summer. ❀ **CULTIVATION** Water well during hot, dry periods and mulch with gravel to prevent the soil from drying out. ❀ **PROPAGATION** From root offsets in winter, or from seed planted in autumn.

Thymus serpyllum
Wild thyme ○ ❖❖❖

✿ **OTHER NAMES** Mother-of-thyme, Thyme
✿ **DESCRIPTION** A delightful, low-growing, evergreen ground cover
that is found growing wild in Europe, western Asia and northern Africa. This
particular species is prized for its ease of cultivation, as well as for its fragrant
foliage and flowers. It can be planted in a herb garden, rockery, or in the
crevices between paving stones, where its perfume can be really enjoyed when
it is walked upon. Spreading quickly as a dense mat of tiny green leaves, it is
covered with terminal clusters of small, rosy-purple flowers for many months,
from spring to autumn. There are several worthwhile varieties, including
'Alba', which has white flowers and 'Coccineus', which has pink flowers.
✿ **PLANTING** Plant in full sun in any moderately rich and well-drained
soil that can hold moisture well during hot, dry weather. Mulch with organic
matter after planting, and water until plants become established and start to
spread. ✿ **FLOWERING** Flowers from spring to autumn, depending on
the warmth of the climate. ✿ **CULTIVATION** Very little maintenance is
necessary once the plants begin to spread. ✿ **PROPAGATION** By
division of clumps in early spring or autumn.

Viola odorata
English violet ◑ ● ❖❖❖

✿ **OTHER NAMES** Violet, Sweet violet ✿ **DESCRIPTION** One of the most popular and easy-to-grow perennials, the sweet violet is a charming addition to any old-fashioned garden, being ideal for the edge of mixed flowerbeds and borders, or as a woodland plant in the shade of deciduous trees. Growing to 8 inches (20 cm) in height, its rhizomatous roots spread through the soil and rapidly cover a large area, making it an excellent ground cover. The dark green, glossy leaves are heart-shaped, while the dainty flowers are borne on slender stems, and can be violet or white in colour. There are many forms and cultivars, including 'Double Russian', which has double, deep purple blooms, and 'Royal Robe', which has purple flowers that are particularly fragrant. ✿ **PLANTING** The soil should be quite rich in humus and well-drained, capable of not drying out completely during hot, dry weather. Plant in autumn, and water well until seeds germinate or divisions take root. ✿ **FLOWERING** Flowers from late winter until mid-spring. ✿ **CULTIVATION** Water well if conditions are hot and dry, and protect foliage from snails and slugs which can be a problem. ✿ **PROPAGATION** Easy to propagate from seed in autumn or spring, or by division of clumps in autumn.

Campanula medium

Canterbury bells ○ ◑

❀ **OTHER NAME** Bellflower ❀ **DESCRIPTION** A delightful, old-fashioned annual for the back of a mixed flowerbed or border, prized for its upright growth and showy flowers in shades of white, blue, and pink. Native to southern Europe, Canterbury bells grow to a height of 4 feet (1.2 m), with strong stems that have a good covering of lance-shaped, toothed, mid-green foliage. The flowers are outstanding, bell-shaped, and either single or double in form. There are many worthwhile cultivars and varieties, including 'Bells of Holland', which has blue, lilac, white, or pink flowers; 'Calycanthema', which has double flowers; and a dwarf form that only grows to 2 feet (60 cm). ❀ **PLANTING** Like most annuals, these fast growers need quite fertile soil to produce good results. Choose a sunny or semi-shaded situation and enrich the soil with plenty of well-rotted organic matter, making sure that there is good drainage. Water seeds lightly but regularly to ensure germination. ❀ **FLOWERING** Flowers appear from late spring until midsummer, depending upon when the seed was sown. ❀ **CULTIVATION** Keep watering regularly, especially during hot or dry weather. A side dressing of general purpose fertilizer will help boost flower production. ❀ **PROPAGATION** From seed sown in autumn for a spring display, or early spring for a summer show.

Centaurea cyanus

Cornflower ○

✿ **OTHER NAMES** Bachelor's button, Blue bottle

✿ **DESCRIPTION** An excellent annual for gardens with poorer soils, the cornflower is easy to grow and requires very little care and attention after it has germinated. Native to the Mediterranean regions of Europe, this annual naturalizes freely, and is even considered a nuisance in some areas. Growing to 2½ feet (76 cm) in height, it has an open habit and lance-shaped, greyish-green foliage. The branching stems carry double, daisy-like, flower heads in various shades of white, pink, purple, or blue. The flowers are good for cutting, and are used frequently by florists. There are dwarf cultivars, including 'Jubilee Gem', which has quite large, dark blue flowers, and 'Polka Dot', which has flowers in shades of blue, pink, and white. ✿ **PLANTING** Seed can be sown in autumn or spring into any well-drained soil. The addition of some well-rotted compost, however, will give better results. Keep the ground moist until the seeds have germinated. ✿ **FLOWERING** Flowers in spring or summer, depending on when the seeds were sown. ✿ **CULTIVATION** Once established little maintenance is required, apart from keeping weeds from around plants and watering if the weather is very hot and dry.

✿ **PROPAGATION** From seed sown in autumn or early spring when frosts have finished.

Clarkia pulchella
Clarkia ○

✿ **OTHER NAME** Rocky mountain garland ✿ **DESCRIPTION** An attractive annual grown for its flowers, which make good cut flowers for indoor arrangements. Native to California, this plant prefers a climate that has cool evenings, and therefore, it will not do well in warm or tropical regions. Growing to 18 inches (45 cm) in height, the stems have lance-shaped, mid-green leaves and showy racemes of flowers in the white to lavender colour range. ✿ **PLANTING** The seeds can be sown directly where they are to grow, in a sunny, open position, then thinned out if too crowded. However, they do look effective in a massed planting, and seem to bloom well when slightly crowded together. The soil should not be over rich, as this will cause foliage growth at the expense of the flowers. Good drainage is important. ✿ **FLOWERING** Flowers bloom from late spring to midsummer, depending on when the seed was sown. ✿ **CULTIVATION** Water well to encourage steady growth, and mulch around the base of plants to keep weed growth down. Do not bring the mulch layer right up to the plant stems. Botrytis can be a problem. ✿ **PROPAGATION** From seed sown in autumn, or early spring in cold regions.

Consolida ambigua (syn. *Delphinium ajacis*)

Larkspur ○

✿ **DESCRIPTION** Generally known as the annual form of delphinium, this delightful plant is another good choice for the cottage garden, blending in with mixed beds of perennials, annuals, and roses. A native of southern Europe, it grows to 2 feet (60 cm) in height, with an excellent covering of feathery, mid-green foliage. The flowers are very striking, and are often used in floral bouquets by florists. They are rounded and spurred, in the violet, pink, rose, and blue colour range. There are giant forms, growing to 4 feet (1.2 m), and also 'Hyacinth-flowered' hybrids, which are a small-growing variety with spikes of tubular flowers that are pink, white, mauve, and blue.

✿ **PLANTING** This fast-growing annual is successful in a wide range of soils and climates, if planted in an open and sunny position. Better results are achieved if the soil has not been overfertilized. Sow seed directly where the plants are to grow. ✿ **FLOWERING** Flowers in late spring or summer, depending on when the seed was sown. ✿ **CULTIVATION** Keep the soil moist until plants have germinated, and water again if conditions become hot or dry. Taller varieties may require staking if planted in an exposed or windy position. ✿ **PROPAGATION** From seed sown in autumn for a spring flowering, or early spring for flowers in summer.

Iberis umbellata
Candytuft ○

✿ **DESCRIPTION** A fast-growing annual that can be mass-planted at
the front of a mixed flowerbed, or grown in any sunny position where white
or mauve flowers are required. A native of southern Europe, the annual
candytuft grows to 1 foot (30 cm) in height, with masses of lance-shaped,
mid-green leaves. The flowers are small and white or mauve, grouped
together in rounded flower heads that give a pretty display. The 'Fairy Series'
of hybrids are slightly smaller in size, with a wonderful array of flowers in
the white, red, pink, and purple colour range. ✿ **PLANTING** The seed
can be sown directly in the ground where the plants are to grow, or raised
to seedling stage in punnets. Autumn and spring are the main planting
times, and the soil should be well prepared with the addition of homemade
compost or general purpose fertilizer. Water well until plants are established,
and mulch to keep weed growth down. ✿ **FLOWERING** Flowers from
late spring to midsummer. ✿ **CULTIVATION** Once established they
should grow quickly without problems. Water if the weather is hot and dry.
✿ **PROPAGATION** From seed sown either in spring or autumn,
depending on when you want them to flower.

Malcolmia maritima
Virginian stock ○

✿ **DESCRIPTION** This old-fashioned favourite is grown for its glorious, fragrant flowers, which make excellent cut flowers. A member of the mustard family, Virginia stock is a fast-growing and easily cultivated annual that reaches 12 inches (30 cm) in height, with attractive lance-shaped, grey-green foliage. The scented flowers, which are borne on spikes, are in the lilac and reddish-to-white colour range. Stock should be grown in a bed close to the house or an outdoor entertaining area, from where its fragrance can be more easily enjoyed. It is a pleasant border plant for the front of a mixed flowerbed, or can be mass-planted to great effect. ✿ **PLANTING** A hardy and durable annual that seems to thrive in most garden soils, providing drainage is adequate. Choose a sunny, open position and incorporate some compost into the ground before sowing the seed or planting out seedlings. Water lightly until the plants become established. ✿ **FLOWERING** Flowers from late spring to midsummer, depending on when the seeds were planted. ✿ **CULTIVATION** Keep weed growth down around plants, and water well if conditions are hot and dry. ✿ **PROPAGATION** From seed sown in spring or summer. Should self-seed readily.

Nemophila menziesii (syn. *Nemophila insignis*)

Baby-blue-eyes ○ ◐

✿ **OTHER NAME** Buffalo eyes ✿ **DESCRIPTION** A useful, fast-growing annual that has a spreading habit and masses of serrated, grey-green leaves. Often planted in rockery gardens, or at the front of a mixed flower border, baby-blue-eyes grows to 2½ feet (76 cm) in height, and has startling, small, bowl-shaped blue flowers with white centres. There are several good varieties, including 'Alba', which has white flowers; 'Grandiflora', which has large, showy blooms; and 'Marginata', which has blue flowers edged with white. ✿ **PLANTING** To give good results, this annual must have quite fertile soil and excellent drainage. Prepare the ground prior to planting with plenty of well-rotted animal manure and compost, and sprinkle a handful of general purpose fertilizer over the soil surface. Seeds can be sown directly where they are to grow, and kept lightly moist until they germinate.
✿ **FLOWERING** Flowers appear from mid-spring until summer.
✿ **CULTIVATION** Mulch to discourage weeds and to help maintain soil moisture during warm weather. Feed with a liquid organic fertilizer as the flower buds are forming. Watch out for aphids, which can attack tender young growth. ✿ **PROPAGATION** From seed sown directly in the ground in early autumn.

Nigella damascena
Love-in-a-mist ○

✿ **DESCRIPTION** A native to southern Europe, this is an easy-to-grow and pretty annual that is a member of the buttercup family. It is a popular and fast-growing species, reaching 18 inches (45 cm) in height, with slender, upright stems clothes in fine, feathery, bright green foliage. The spurred flowers are small but showy, in semi-doubles of blue, pink, and white. Worthwhile varieties include 'Miss Jekyll blue', which has semi-double, blue flowers, and 'Persian Jewels', which has white, pink, or purple-blue flowers. The flowers are followed by decorative seed pods, which can be allowed to dry to provide seed for the following season. ✿ **PLANTING** This annual grows well in most soils and climates, providing drainage is adequate. Add some organic matter to the ground prior to sowing the seeds, and kept the area lightly moist until germination. ✿ **FLOWERING** Flowers during late spring and early summer. ✿ **CULTIVATION** Weed around the young seedlings as they grow, and mulch to help keep the soil moist. Deadheading will encourage more flowers to be produced. ✿ **PROPAGATION** In cool climates seed is sown in spring when the danger of frost has passed; in other regions, seed is sown in autumn.

Phlox drummondii

Annual phlox ○ ◑

❀ **OTHER NAMES** Drummond phlox

❀ **DESCRIPTION** A delightful, moderately fast-growing and bushy annual that can be used as part of a flowerbed or border, or planted in a container to give a splash of colour on a patio or balcony. Growing to 18 inches (45 cm) in height, it develops a pleasant shape of lance-shaped, light green leaves. The flower heads are prolific, in the cream, pink, and red colour range, sometimes with contrasting centres. There are many attractive varieties that have even larger and more showy flowers, including the Twinkle Series, and 'Tretras'. The form 'Petticoat' has very pretty bicoloured flowers.

❀ **PLANTING** Phlox need fertile, well-drained soil to grow successfully, and they can be situated either in full sun or partial shade. Clear the ground of weeds, and add some general purpose fertilizer prior to sowing the seed. Keep lightly watered until germination. ❀ **FLOWERING** Flowers from summer through to autumn, depending on when the seed was sown.

❀ **CULTIVATION** Protect young plants from snails and slugs, and side-dress every four weeks to maintain steady growth. ❀ **PROPAGATION** From seed sown in autumn or spring, depending on the climate.

Primula malacoides
Fairy primrose

♣ **DESCRIPTION** A tidy, clump-forming perennial, most commonly grown as an annual because it dislikes cold winters. In cold climates it can be grown in a greenhouse. Growing to 18 inches (45 cm) in height, it is a very popular plant that originated in China, but is now grown successfully in many parts of the world. The soft, pale green foliage has a hairy texture, while the flowers appear in dense whorls that cover it entirely for many weeks. The flowers are small, single or double in form, and in the white, pink, purple, and carmine colour range. An outstanding cultivar is 'Gilham's White', which has a good display of pure-white flowers. ♣ **PLANTING** The soil for this species of primula must be rather gritty and well-drained, and a semi-shade is preferable. The seed should be sown in autumn for a spring flowering, and the ground kept lightly damp until germination is successful. ♣ **FLOWERING** Flowers from spring onwards, depending on when the seed was sown. ♣ **CULTIVATION** Take care not to allow the soil to dry out completely, but do not overwater. Weed around young plants as they grow. ♣ **PROPAGATION** From seed sown in autumn.

Salvia splendens
Scarlet sage ○ ◑

✿ **DESCRIPTION** A vigorous although slow-growing perennial that is generally grown as an annual because it is frost tender. A native of Brazil, it grows to 2 feet (60 cm) in height, and can be used as part of a mixed flowerbed or border, planted towards the centre. It can also be mass-planted for a colourful, late summer display. The bright green foliage is oval with serrated edges, covered with showy racemes of scarlet flowers in late summer and autumn. There are many attractive varieties, including 'Fireworks', which has red and white striped flowers, and 'Flare Path', which has dramatic, scarlet flowers. ✿ **PLANTING** In hot climates this salvia appreciates some shade in the middle of the day, otherwise it can be planted in full sun in fertile, well-drained loam that has been enriched with plenty of compost or manure. Water lightly until seeds germinate. ✿ **FLOWERING** Flowers in late summer and autumn. ✿ **CULTIVATION** Mulch around the plant as it grows, to help prevent the soil from drying out in summer. It will continue to grow until killed by frost. ✿ **PROPAGATION** From seed sown in early spring when the danger of frost has passed.

Senecio x *hybridus*
Cineraria ○

✿ **DESCRIPTION** A handsome annual that is probably the parent of the popular and brightly coloured cinerarias that we see in florist shops today. A native of the Canary Islands, this charming plant grows to 18 inches (45 cm) in height, with large oval leaves that are carried on short, woolly stems. The flowers are very eye-catching and are the main reason for growing this particular species. They are large and daisy-like in the red to purple colour range. It can also be grown as a bedding plant where summer colour is required. There are many hybrid forms (*Senecio* x *hybridus*), which are grown as annuals, and are well worth cultivating for their dramatic flowers.

✿ **PLANTING** Prepare the soil well with plenty of organic matter, because this cineraria likes quite fertile, moist, and well-drained growing conditions. Full sun will give the best results. Seed can be sown in early spring, and mulched when seedlings have reached 6 inches (15 cm) in height.

✿ **FLOWERING** Flowers appear in mid to late summer, depending on the warmth of the climate. ✿ **CULTIVATION** Water well, especially during hot and dry periods. Keep weeds from around the base of plants, but avoid disturbing the root run. ✿ **PROPAGATION** From seed sown in spring.

INDEX OF BOTANICAL NAMES

INDEX OF COMMON NAMES

INDEX OF COMMON NAMES

PHOTOGRAPHY CREDITS

The Garden Picture Library: p.10 (Brigitte Thomas), p.11 (John Sims), p.12 (David Russell), p.15 (John Glover), p.16 (Gary Rogers), p.18 (John Glover), p.21 (Brian Carter), p.22 (Brian Carter), p.24 (Anthony Paul), p. 26 (Didier Willery), p.28 (Wolfram Stehling), p. 29 (John Glover), p.30 (John Glover), p.31 (John Glover), p.35 (Brian Carter), p.42 (Didier Willery), p.46 (Linda Burgess), p.50 (Neil Homes), p.53 (John Glover), p.54 (John Glover), p.55 (JS Sira), p.61 (C. Fairweather), p.72, p.79 (John Glover), p.90 (John Glover), p.92 (John Glover), p.93 (Brian Carter), p.96 (Brian Carter), p.98 (Robert Estall), p.99 (Brian Carter), p.100 (Brian Carter), p.101 (Marijke Heuff), front cover and p.102 (LindaBurgess), p. 104 Marijke Heuff); **Ivy Hansen Photography:** p.20, p.34, p.26, p.37, p.38, p.39, p.41, p.43, p.47, p.48, p.56, p.57, p.58, p.59, p.60, p.63, p.65, p.66, p.70, p.71, p.73, p.76, p.80, p.82, p.85, p.86, p.89, p.91, p.94, p.97, p.99, p.103, p.105, p.106, p.107, p.108, p.109; **S & O Mathews:** p.13, p.17, p.19, p.23, p.25, p.27, p.40, p.45, p.49, p.51, p.52, p.74, p.81, p.83, p.88; **Clive Nichols:** p.44, p.67, p.78; **Photo/Nats:** p.32; **Lorna Rose:** p.14, p.33, p.62, p.64, p.71, p.75, p.77, p.84, p.87, p.95; **Lansdowne Publishing:** p.68